GROUP

A COMPREHENSIVE BLUEPRINT

COACHING

GROUP COACHING

A COMPREHENSIVE BLUEPRINT

GINGER COCKERHAM, MCC

iUniverse, Inc.
Bloomington

Group Coaching
A Comprehensive Blueprint

Copyright © 2011 Ginger Cockerham, MCC

All rights reserved. No part of this book may be used or reproduced by any means, graphic, electronic, or mechanical, including photocopying, recording, taping or by any information storage retrieval system without the written permission of the publisher except in the case of brief quotations embodied in critical articles and reviews.

iUniverse books may be ordered through booksellers or by contacting:

iUniverse
1663 Liberty Drive
Bloomington, IN 47403
www.iuniverse.com
1-800-Authors (1-800-288-4677)

Because of the dynamic nature of the Internet, any web addresses or links contained in this book may have changed since publication and may no longer be valid. The views expressed in this work are solely those of the author and do not necessarily reflect the views of the publisher, and the publisher hereby disclaims any responsibility for them.

ISBN: 978-1-4502-9067-8 (sc)
ISBN: 978-1-4502-9068-5 (e)

Printed in the United States of America

iUniverse rev. date: 2/25/2011

Dedication

This book is dedicated to Beth Lyons. Beth and I have been collaborating in group coaching since 2004. We co-created the learning guides for the ICF accredited programs at the Power of Groups at Coachville and for an Israeli school Gome. We are both excited about everything that is 'group coaching'.

Acknowledgments

I would like to acknowledge the people who made it possible for this book to be finished. Thanks to my Virtual Assistant, Kathryn Whipple, who headed up the book team. She kept the faith and worked so hard to help me reach the finish line, and to my friend Jan Moore for her editing, impeccable taste, and feedback.

A special thanks to Zuno Kristal, who has been my friend and advocate at Columbia University and co-instructor of the group coaching course there. To Dave Buck who supported and collaborated with me to create the Power of Groups Community, to my great coach and fellow Clue Sister, Judy Feld, and to Dr. Terry Malbia for holding the torch for group coaching at Teachers College Columbia University.

To my biggest fan and number one supporter, my husband Steve. A special acknowledgement to our four incredible children, Stephen, Courtney, Casey and Ginny, and our wonderful grandchildren, Chris, Caroline, and Will Rader, Kate, Maggie, and Emma Cockerham, and to Jacob, Ethan, Austin, and Luke Cohen. I am the most grateful woman to have the love and support of such a wonderful family.

Contents

About the Book		vii
Introduction		ix
Chapter One:	Group Coaching Defined	1
Chapter Two:	Focus from Passion and Vision	7
Chapter Three:	Building Social Capital	14
Chapter Four:	Confidential Connections	25
Chapter Five:	Active Listening in a Coaching Group	35
Chapter Six:	Laser Speaking-Everyone in the Conversation	47
Chapter Seven:	Powerful Questioning in a Group	55
Chapter Eight:	Full Group Engagement	63
Chapter Nine:	Collaborative Agendas-Group Based Content	70
Chapter Ten:	Championing the Group	78
Chapter Eleven:	Laser Coaching	86
Chapter Twelve:	Creating Awareness	93
Chapter Thirteen:	Eliminating Energy Drains	101
Chapter Fourteen:	Return on Investment	113
Chapter Fifteen:	Marketing Group Coaching	125
Chapter Sixteen:	Designing a Group Coaching Business	134
About the Author		141

About the Book

Group Coaching: A Comprehensive Blueprint focuses on how a professional coach can create a successful and sustainable business by coaching groups. Group coaching can be offered to peers who are in quest of the same goal or objective, and to companies and organizations seeking to leverage and expand coaching environments to achieve organizational initiatives. Below are the advantages and benefits of reading this book.

You will receive:

- Conceptual Clarity: Definition of key terms and distinctions between group coaching and traditional methods of leading and facilitating for teams and groups.

- Coaching Foundation: How to establish the International Coach Federation Core Competencies as the foundation for facilitating and coaching groups.

- Applied Action: Skills, tools, and processes for developing and enhancing group coaching expertise.

- Marketing Strategies: Using your advocates to help you collect and attract ongoing coaching groups.

Benefits:

- Learn how to design groups based on a coaching model. This will help you create an environment of collaboration and co-creation that will enhance creativity and success.

- Explore multiple group coaching case studies and models from experienced coaches, who coach teams and groups worldwide. You will receive insider information on what works well in group coaching from experienced group coaches.

- Integrate the core coaching competencies that are essential for creating viable and long-lasting groups.

- Build a model for creating and sustaining your own group coaching business. You will be able to replicate a successful model for ongoing coaching groups.

- Expand the reach and relevance of your coaching groups in the marketplace. This keeps your groups current and marketable to your ideal clients.

- Develop proven marketing strategies for collecting internal and external coaching groups. This will help you expand the market for your group business.

Introduction

> *"A recent study estimates that 40,000 people in the U.S. work as coaches (work or life) and the $2.4 billion market is growing at a fast-paced 18% per year."*
> —MarketData Report, 2009

This book was written as a celebration of the creation and development of the coaching industry since the early 1990s. Coaching has spread across the globe as a force for personal and professional growth and achievement and continues to grow at an amazing rate. This book focuses specifically on the art and skill of coaching peer groups.

The International Coach Federation (ICF), which has over eighteen thousand members worldwide, defines professional coaching as an "ongoing professional relationship that helps people produce extraordinary results in their lives, careers, businesses, or organizations." Through the process of coaching, clients deepen their learning, improve their performance, and enhance their quality of life. The definition continues: "With each meeting, the client chooses the focus of conversation, while the coach listens and contributes observations and questions. This interaction creates clarity and moves the client into action. Coaching accelerates the client's progress by providing greater focus and awareness of choice. Coaching concentrates on where clients are now and what they are willing to do to get where they want to be in the future."

I was an early adopter of coaching as a profession. In 1995 I heard Thomas Leonard, one of the founders of the coaching industry, say, "I have a vision that coaching will go around the world and change the way people communicate and interact forever." At that moment, I knew I wanted to be a part of that vision and that I would do what it took to become a full-time coach and spend the rest of my professional life coaching people. I joined Coach University that year and graduated from their coaching program in 1997. I transitioned out of my real estate tax business and became a full-time coach that same year.

My first group coaching program started that year, when I was sponsored by an executive who was my client in a major financial services company. This program launched in 1997 with two groups, and the results were so promising that the groups were renewed and expanded in 1998. I continued to coach financial services professionals individually and in groups. In 2007 I wrote a book with a fellow coach and financial professional, Diane Dixon, titled *Magnificent Masters in Financial Services*. The book features fourteen successful women in the financial services industry and highlights their models for success. It provides templates for women who are interested in becoming financial advisors to help them establish their own businesses. Several of the fourteen women featured in the book were members of the early coaching groups.

Since that first experience in 1997 as a coach of groups, I knew the group model was how I wanted to build my coaching business. I have coached many groups internally with companies and have also attracted individual professionals into my external groups. I have focused on coaching groups for over fourteen years. I have discovered that group coaching helps companies achieve organizational goals by increasing individual performance. Group coaching also enhances individual growth and development, which leads to greater satisfaction and retention of key employees and producers.

In the last fifteen years I have received my Master Certified Coach designation through ICF, served on the International Coach Federation Global Board of Directors, and was the vice president of the organization for two years. I currently serve on the board of trustees for the ICF Foundation. The foundation provides resources to outstanding educational programs worldwide. Teaching group coaching has become a passion for me. Along with Beth Lyons, I have created the group coaching curriculum for the Coachville Power of Groups, the Columbia University Group Coaching Course, and for the Israeli school Gome. All of these group coaching programs are ICF accredited CCEU programs.

While group coaching collects and connects people who choose to be a part of the group, team coaching focuses on enrolling an intact team. That distinction between choice and enrollment is an important one. To gain more knowledge of the distinctions between team coaching and group coaching, I encourage you to read the article titled "Expansion: scaling the benefits of coaching for groups and teams," in *Choice* magazine, volume 6, number 4, by Ginger Cockerham, MCC, and DJ Mitsch, MCC. Examples of coaching groups include executive peer groups for managing innovation and change, independent sales professionals in an affiliated company, and managers integrating coaching skills to create effective employee performance.

There is an art to coaching groups that is based on the understanding that the most valuable role coaches can play in groups is to show up as the coach of the group collectively and as the coach for each of the group members individually. Even though coaches step into the role of facilitator, mentor, and teacher, these roles are not a coach's primary role. Our highest and best use is to be in a fully partnered coaching relationship with the group collectively.

Coaching in a peer group can facilitate group members to make the changes, shifts, and leaps that are necessary for them to move from what is not working in their business or their lives and move forward confidently with purpose and momentum. A masterful coach can be instrumental in helping clients gain the insight and awareness necessary for making significant changes and incredible leaps toward their goals and dreams. This is not to discount the valuable contribution that members play in this process. When group members share their experiences, knowledge, and insights, their wisdom and experience can be a catalyst in a transformational process.

Group coaching also offers group members the opportunity to have an accountability system around them that motivates them to achieve their goals. One group member said, "I have been working to attain this level of production and success for over twelve years, and after joining our coaching group, I was able to reach the goal in the first year."

Group Coaching: A Comprehensive Blueprint focuses on the group coaching process to help coaches create effective and sustainable coaching groups for years to come.

Chapter One
Group Coaching Defined

"Coming together, ordinary people can perform extraordinary feats. They can push things that come into their hands a little higher up, a little further on toward the heights of excellence."
—Unknown

Group coaching is a facilitated group process led by a skilled professional coach and created with the intention of maximizing the combined energy, experience, and wisdom of individuals who choose to join in order to achieve organizational objectives or individual goals. Groups and teams are how initiatives are accomplished in companies and organizations.

Examples of coaching groups:

- Entrepreneurial business owners who want to work as CEOs by working more on their businesses than in their businesses.
- Executive peer groups that encourage innovation and change within their companies or organizations.

- Sales professionals with independent offices and affiliated with the same company.
- Executive women leaders in international organizations.
- Managers integrating coaching skills for leading and facilitating effective teams.
- Individuals wanting to change and enhance their lives.

Team Coaching

Team coaching is a facilitated process where participants are enrolled by a team leader (usually the team's manager or a project lead) for a specific intention related to accomplishing goals or milestones. A team with a coaching approach is focused on the team's overall win and what it takes for each individual to contribute to the team's win. The focus is on what the team needs versus individual wants.

Examples of team coaching:

- Sales teams (both high-performing teams that need to stretch or low-performing teams that need a boost)
- Leadership teams (CEOs, division heads) setting strategies
- Global work teams (often virtual)

D. J. Mitsch from the *Choice* magazine article titled "Expansion: scaling the benefits of coaching for groups and teams," wrote, "Hierarchies on teams can be predetermined with preset roles, such as: team manager, timekeeper, note-taker, facilitator, etc. Team members are often required to bring their skill set to the team in order to accomplish a team goal."

Group Coaching and Facilitation

Coaching
Focuses on the individual's experience: "What is your need? What do you want? What is missing?" The coaching focus is primarily on the people and their experiences, and not on a process or an agenda.

Facilitating
A tool used to focus on the process. Facilitation ensures a smooth flow, allowing everyone his or her say. It is process and agenda-oriented.

Group Coach and Consulting

Coaching
Creates and evokes collaborative value, evoking the shared wisdom and experience from within the group, rather than striving to provide external "solutions." The coach is generally considered to be an expert in coaching and group process, not a specific industry expert.

Consulting
Uses various tools and methods to analyze and advise. The consultant is generally considered to be an expert in the specific situation or subject. Consulting is solution-driven rather than focused on personal and professional development.

Group Coaching and Teleclass Leading

Coaching
Coaching focuses on the individual and "just in time" issues, with participants determining the agenda. Coaching groups have a predetermined beginning date but can experience long-term bonding, with some groups lasting several years before they end.

Teleclass Leading
Driven by content and information, teleclasses have predetermined beginning and ending dates. The teleclass leader has expertise in the content and in teaching methodology.

Group Coaching and Advising

Coaching
Coaches provide skill sets that enable participants to depend upon themselves to ascertain answers. Coaching trusts the group process and recognizes that the participants are their own most valuable resource for experience and expertise.

Advising
An advisor is typically brought in to give recommendations based on his or her personal experience. For example, accountants who give advice about financial investments will presume highly specific, predetermined scenarios and dispense investment advice to the group in general. By contrast, a coach specializing in the financial area might work with the same client group to help them clarify their personal

investment goals and identify strategies and actions steps to successfully reach those goals.

Group Coaching vs. Mentoring

Coaching
Coaches help participants create their own models of success based on the individual person's strengths and choices.

Mentoring
A group mentor has been on the same career or development path as the group participants and shares and guides others based on the mentor's model of success. They can be invaluable to professionals new to an industry to help navigate efficiently through the learning curve and to get support and encouragement from a mentor who can share her or his own experiences.

Advanced coaching skills are required for coaching in a group. It is exciting for experienced coaches to meet the challenge of expanding their coaching business to include groups. If the intention is for individual group and team members to experience the same kind of impact and transformation that our one-to-one coaching clients experience, coaches must perfect and apply advanced coaching skills. This book is designed as a guide for coaches who coach groups or who want to expand their coaching into the group coaching arena.

In order to be effective as a group coach, it is helpful to start with an understanding of the value group coaching brings to the group members. There is real power and passion in creating a group coaching environment. Coaching groups are formed to achieve organizational initiatives as well as individual goals. That process is made possible by the combination of group members, who join the group by choice and who identify a clear mission and goals they want to achieve along with a professional who is their coach and guide through the process.

With clarity of purpose, each member commits to take the actions necessary to reach their goals and complete their mission. In the process, they tap into the collective energy, experience, and wisdom that are held within the group. As a result, the individuals are encouraged and inspired to commit to moving forward, then to take the action steps they have identified as necessary to achieve their goals, and to excel in the supportive environment of a coaching group. As a result, they gain coaching tools and resources, new perspectives and awareness, insight and clarity, and inspiration and momentum while they follow their action plan and take responsibility for achieving the results they want.

Trusting the Group Process

In order to have very successful coaching groups, it's vital that you are comfortable with and trust the group process itself. As a coach, you will create an environment that facilitates the process and apply the tools to help you tweak it and grow it. However, you are not in control of the process. This means that the participants choose how the group operates in concert with you as the coach. This book is dedicated to helping you become a masterful group coach so that you can support the group members achieve great things. And central to all of this is that you can trust that coaching works, and a group of peers bring great wisdom.

For a new group coach this can be an adjustment. It's a little like trying to drive a car without being in direct control of either the steering wheel or the gas pedal. It can be scary in the beginning.

Trusting the group process is much easier to understand if you've had the opportunity to contribute in a group or if you currently are experiencing the benefits of group participation yourself.

Beth Lyons, www.techiecoach.com

bethmlyons@gmail.com

The group coaching experience is fairly unique in today's world. It's unusual to be part of a group where people give each other their full attention, listen deeply, tell each other the truth, share their heartfelt dreams and goals, support each other in moving forward, and celebrate achieving success. Add to this a coach skilled in creating a coaching environment and building the skills that allow those things to happen, and what you offer to people is an experience that is rare and very valuable.

Peer wisdom and accountability are key advantages of group participation. A powerful example of this is how a creative genius was able to stay the course as his mastery developed with the help of his artist's group.

Bruce Eric Kaplan, longtime cartoonist with *The New Yorker* magazine, said in a National Public Radio interview that he loved to draw little cartoon people as a child and dreamed of becoming a cartoonist. He had the dream, but it was just a dream until he joined with others to support him. In pursuit of his dream, he joined a creative artist's group in New York in his late twenties. To remain a part of this group, he was required to make creative commitments, produce each week, and support others in reaching their dreams. His commitment to the group was to draw ten cartoon frames each week. Instead of filing them away, he decided to send them to his "dream" magazine, *The New Yorker*. For the next two and a half years he sent cartoon frames to the magazine each week, despite the fact that the cartoons were returned to him with an unsigned, impersonal rejection card.

Instead of giving up, Bruce never wavered in his persistence. In fact, he started sending notes each week with expletives interspersed, saying that any other "bleeping" magazine in the world would be printing these great cartoons. The support and encouragement of his creative group reassured and buoyed his confidence through continual rejection. He continued to produce because of his group.

When Bruce returned to his apartment one day to discover a FedEx envelope from *The New Yorker*, he immediately started crying with relief just knowing that someone had been reading his cartoons. When he called the magazine as directed, the editor told Bruce that he and the staff had been reading his cartoons all along but that they were waiting for him to be ready for publication.

Since 1991, Bruce Kaplan's cartoons are featured regularly in *The New Yorker*. Bruce perfected his art and craft, and over that two-and-a-half-year period he was able to stay the course with the support and motivation of his creative artists' group.

Coaching Questions

1. What are three group experiences that have been very beneficial to you?
2. What were the characteristics of those groups that contributed to making it a positive and beneficial experience for you?
3. Note three group experiences you've had that were not helpful for you.
4. What were the characteristics that prevented them from being helpful?
5. What can you take from your own experiences that can make your coaching groups better?

Chapter Two
Focus from Passion and Vision

"Alone we can do so little; together we can do so much."
—Estill I. Green, VP of Bell Telephone Laboratory

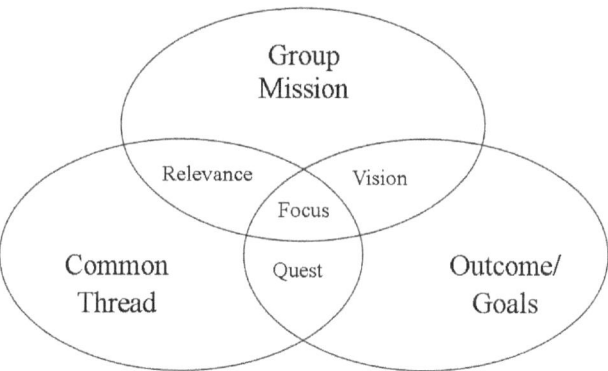

After coaching my first group and deciding that coaching groups would be an integral part of my coaching business, I started a quest for creating content that I thought would be so exciting that I could market it to companies and individuals who would flock to my group offerings. I spent hours sitting at the computer, developing the programs that had the keys for creating life balance, building referral engines, or designing systems that would streamline financial services offices nationwide.

I soon discovered that creating what I thought were wonderful programs in the vacuum of my own office was a complete waste of time in the marketplace. When no one else thought these programs were interesting enough to buy or show up for, I quickly learned that I needed to focus on what others wanted—not what I thought they wanted.

Choosing a Focus

There are many ways to choose a focus for your groups. One of the easiest and most effective ways is to choose a focus based on a **shared passion**.

A coach who completed the 2006 *12 Keys Mentoring Program*, a group coaching program that I have offered to experienced coaches since 2001, has a passion for preserving and protecting the environment by "going green" in her life and her business. After she became part of a networking community of like-minded environmentalists who were on the same path she was, she found that many business owners wanted to go green in their businesses but didn't have the knowledge, support, and accountability to implement their intentions. As she grew her social capital within circles of others inspired by the green movement and increased her expertise in sustainability, she became inspired to coach groups in that arena. The more she spoke on the subject and highlighted her desire to help others on the same journey, the more she was able to attract entrepreneurial business owners to join her coaching groups. As she fulfilled her desire to create a more environmentally safe planet, she was also able to make her business more successful and sustainable by filling her coaching groups.

Another great way to choose a focus is by reaching out and discovering a *vital need* that your ideal clients have. Once the need is identified, then groups can be created to help them meet those needs. For example, if the economy is down and people are being laid off from their jobs, it would be natural to engage job seekers or career changers in a conversation, survey, teleforum, or presentation to find out what would be most valuable and helpful as they navigate through change. A coach and group can offer support, encouragement, and accountability through the process of finding employment.

If you have experience as a career coach or consultant, this would be a natural niche. Even if you have no experience in this arena, if you have a passion for learning how to navigate the job-loss waters and have the enthusiasm and energy to research, interview, and discover all you need to know to be a great coach for "career changers," this could create successful groups. The key piece is to be open to collaborate with your potential clients to create value and results.

I created a group coaching business out of a passion to leverage the coaching experience for financial services professionals and making it scalable in companies and organizations. In the *12 Keys Program*, I have mentored hundreds of coaches to develop their own coaching groups by identifying the ideal clients they love to coach. I have a vision that coaching groups will be the standard in companies for achieving organizational success while bringing personal growth and peer support for leaders, managers, and employees.

Another way to create a group focus is to tap into another person's vision. One of my executive clients had a vision that in the male-dominated industry where she works, that thousands of women in the future would establish successful financial services businesses and experience the success and satisfaction that she has had in her own business. This was in 1997, and she described a frustrating current reality where outstanding women were recruited into the company where she had been a producer for over twenty years, and the majority of these women were leaving their positions within the first five years. Because she had found coaching so valuable personally, she let me know she believed if more women were coached in those first five years the retention rate would improve greatly.

She suggested that we start coaching groups for the women relatively new to the business so that they would have a professional coach and a community of peers who could relate to and support them in establishing a financial practice. She suggested that the group model would be more appealing for her company's buy-in because of the reduced cost of coaching more individuals in a group and the potential for quicker results. As a result of this leader's initiative and the foresight of decision makers in the organization, we launched a pilot program of two coaching groups for women who had been in the business from three to five years. In the next three years, these groups expanded to ten groups. In the first three years, the retention rate in the company went up 300%. The women in the coaching groups very seldom left the business. That group coaching initiative continues today as the retention rate as well as the success rate of women producers within the company has continued to increase progressively.

After choosing an ideal client, the next step for a coach is to identify a compelling mission and focus for the group members. Using a survey, a questionnaire, or an interview process with potential clients are great ways for gleaning the information needed to discover needs, gaps, and desires of these clients. The key to getting participation in the survey, questionnaire, or interview is to construct questions that are relevant and can be answered quickly and effortlessly.

Example of Three-Part Interview Form

This is a three-part interview form I have used when putting groups together. My goal was to interview five ideal clients, women and men who were well-established financial services professionals. One of the keys to successful interviews is to assure busy professionals that the interview will take less than twenty minutes.

Information
- How long have you been in the financial services industry?
- What has been the most rewarding part of this business for you?
- Who has been most influential in your success?
- Who are your ideal clients?

Obstacles
- Name three things in your business you would like to upgrade.
- What is missing from your office or team?
- What is the most frustrating part of your business?
- Do you have adequate life balance?

Vision
- On what part of your business would you like to spend 70% of your time?
- What difference would you experience if your time was put to the highest and best use?
- Are you using your strengths to be the CEO of your company?
- What do you need in your business to be extraordinarily successful?
- What is the greatest value clients tell you that you give to them?

In completing the interview process, I always ask if I can have a very brief follow-up conversation for clarity and additional questions that have come up in the process. The follow-up conversation gives me a chance to continue the conversation in hopes of getting them invested in the idea of the value of collaborating and sharing with their peers.

After the interview, I had much more clarity on what the focus of the group would be and who might be interested in being part of that process. I follow the interviews with an invitation to all who have participated in the survey or interviews to come to a teleforum where key peer information will be shared. I also encourage them to invite their peers who have not participated. In fact, I send an invitation to join the teleforum that they can forward to their industry peers. This is a cost-free experience that gives everyone the opportunity to participate.

The overall idea of finding a coaching focus from a shared passion and vision is to help narrow the broad concept of unlimited potential coaching groups to something specific enough that you have a general idea of who would be in them. Or at least narrow it enough that you know with whom you would start the conversation.

Once you have this coaching focus, you can start interviewing people and gathering information that will help you understand what the vital need is that the group would address.

Even if you're building a group around one of your passions, it's still important to have conversations and interviews with the potential clients who would be in your group. Not only is this a great way to create awareness and get the word out, it's also important that the creation of this group is much bigger than you could imagine by yourself. This is a pitfall that new group coaches can fall into. Understanding your own interest and passion around a focus doesn't mean that group members won't have other concerns, interests, and ideas that are very different from yours yet in the same arena. Turn your passion into inquiry and build a group around your understanding of the shared passion, which you develop through the collaborative survey and interview process.

This way you also set the stage for group members to be co-creators and contributors from the start. They can become your research and development team, and they create the group with you (whether or not they actually join it). Often people who feel engaged with you in this process will recommend the group to others if they don't feel it's the right time for them.

Turning a passion into coaching groups

Beth Lyons's first coaching group was designed to help people achieve a specific dream. It was based on Barbara Sher's *Teamworks* model, and she specifically put it together to make sure she had some personal support in deciding whether or not to start a coaching business. This group met for more than four years, and while their individual goals changed over time, they shared a passion for helping each other achieve their dreams. Their need for support and a community where their dreams were taken seriously remained central throughout our time together. This model that Beth was certified to lead was a great launching opportunity for her coaching groups.

One coach asked me if there is such a thing as too broad a focus for a group. I replied, "Absolutely!" One of my favorite sayings is, "Market specifically and coach generally." It is important that the focus is specific enough that your ideal clients have no hesitation in joining the group. After you have interviewed them and identified their specific needs and wants, you have the opportunity to tailor your group coaching offering to them specifically. You have engaged them in the process of co-creating a group focus that the majority of participants identify with. Once you have that much input and confirmation, you can feel confident in creating flyers and other marketing materials to send to all the people in this network. As you begin your own groups, start by identifying the passions you have and the social capital you have with people in a specific focus group.

Case Study with a Recruiter Group

In 1998, after coaching groups in two financial services companies, I got a call from a financial recruiter, who told me that she was a member of an intact group of recruiters who wanted to hire a coach for the group. She asked if I would be willing to be interviewed by the group, and I immediately answered, "Of course." We met on a telephone conference bridge, since these recruiters were in financial agencies located across the country. They had met at a national convention of a recruiter's association. One of the first questions they asked me was what I could teach them to help them become more effective recruiters. I responded that their collective knowledge about recruiting was impressive, and since I had no experience in recruiting, I would depend on them to bring that knowledge to the group.

I then explained how I, as their coach, would listen actively, ask powerful and curious questions, and through this inquiry process help them evoke a new awareness and understanding of what they are doing now and how they could step up their game to be more effective and accountable in the actions they take. The group interviewed three coaches, and they hired me immediately despite my lack of experience in their arena. I coached the group for two years, and they achieved the results they wanted as well as improving the quality of their lives.

Coaching Questions

1. Who is your favorite client, and how would you feel about coaching a group of seven of your favorite clients?
2. What do your ideal clients say they value most about you as a coach?
3. What is the most common need your prospects share with you?
4. What is the most satisfying shift or change a client has ever made while working with you?
5. What would you want your legacy in group coaching to be?

Chapter Three
Building Social Capital

"The new economy is not just about the exchange of information; it's about the exchange of relationships."
—Pam Alexander, CEO Alexander Ogilvy Public Relations Worldwide, *Fast Company Magazine*, March 2001

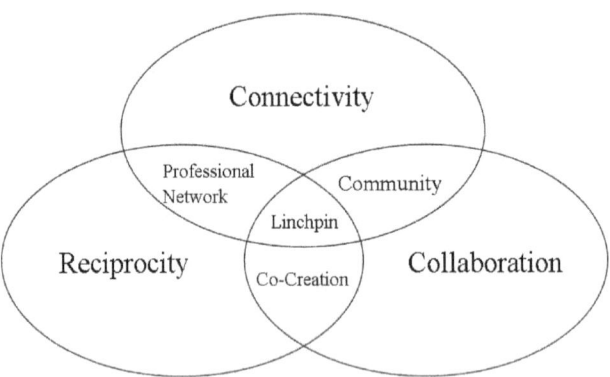

The idea of social capital is very different from what we typically think of when we say "networking." My favorite model for creating social capital comes from Dr. Wayne Baker and his book, *Achieving Success Through Social Capital*. His premise is based on the concept of reciprocity. The idea is that as we give generously in the world and in our community, that generosity is returned to us. It exemplifies the principle of giving and receiving equally.

The reality of most networking efforts as practiced in business is making a connection with people in order to get something from them. Dr. Baker's social capital model involves connecting with others in order to contribute something of value to the group. In this social capital model, the process is outward focused rather than inward focused.

Dr. Baker talks about the concept of reciprocity in creating a community that is all about giving and receiving. Reverend Billy Graham said, "God has given us two hands, one to receive with and the other to give with." Giving and receiving is a fair-trade model that strengthens and encourages long-term social connections. This concept is a much different way of approaching networking than the traditional marketing approach.

As I built my group coaching business, I thought about the graduate course I had taken in marketing at Colorado State and almost broke out in hives thinking about how I would have to develop a thirty-five-page plan for marketing groups to individuals, organizations, and associations. It was only after I changed my perspective in this area that I was able to be effective in filling groups. The first step I took was to change my language to collecting groups.

Collecting Community

My shift in thinking was to focus on what I loved to do and where I excelled, rather than developing a standard marketing strategy. I discovered that I had always enjoyed collecting community and sharing within a community of generous and loving people. I decided that instead of marketing my groups, I would collect people and invite them to become a part of my group coaching vision. Once I made that shift, I was able to create an exciting plan that included the collecting strategies that I enjoyed doing and how they would be effective in attracting my ideal clients. Many of the coaches in my mentoring program have shifted their language from marketing to a word or phrase that is more comfortable to them. For example, many use words like "attracting," "inviting," "engaging," or "inspiring."

One of my favorite stories about collecting a community of advocates is the story of a great Olympic athlete, Bonnie Blair, the speed skater. Bonnie made US Olympic history after becoming the first American athlete, male or female, to win five gold medals in the winter Olympics. Her unflappable and relaxed demeanor distinguished her during the Games. How did she remain relaxed under such extraordinary pressure? In an interview with ABC's John McKay, Bonnie said that one of the keys for winning was surrounding herself with a community of coaches, friends, and family at the Games.

Blair's loyal circle of friends came to every Olympic city where she competed. The Blair bunch was forty-five members strong in Albertville, France in 1992, when they all linked arms at the Games and sang "My Bonnie Lies Over the Ocean" moments before Blair skated onto the ice.

More than sixty members of Blair's bunch traveled to Lillehammer, Norway, in 1994, where Bonnie made Olympic history winning her fifth gold medal. McKay asked her if all the people accompanying her didn't actually distract her and add additional pressure that might affect her focus and performance. Bonnie said, "No way! I love their support and encouragement." She added, "They didn't come just to see me win. They would have come to support me anyway, because we love to be together and have fun."

Creating a community to support and advocate for you is something that will not only help you create success with group coaching, but will also give you the support and encouragement you may need to stay the course in business development. It is also in this community where you can create a rich and satisfying life. The great thing about social capital is that it is a reciprocal model. So as you create rich social capital to build your group coaching business, you also have the opportunity to help others in your circle achieve their dreams.

A great exercise is to visualize an entrepreneurial network with you standing in the middle of hundreds of like-minded people. This concept has been the catalyst for the thousands of online communities and a key for the campaign engine that helped elected Barack Obama president of the United States. His website, Organizing for America, along with multiple other websites, engaged many people who had not participated in the election process before.

Networking is typically more successful for extroverts, who are comfortable meeting new people and interacting in social gatherings. Social capital, on the other hand, allows introverts as well as extroverts an opportunity to participate in communities. Online networking allows people from all over the globe to tap into a reservoir of like-minded people. The visual below is a good tool for examining the depth and breadth of your own social capital. These concentric circles are a visual representation of all the people you know and have interacted with.

Expanding Community

Dr. Baker says that the ability to connect, collaborate, cooperate, and reciprocate is a key factor in distinguishing us as humans. Expanding communities for making contributions to others allows us to experience the joy of close relationships as we engage in building social capital for our business.

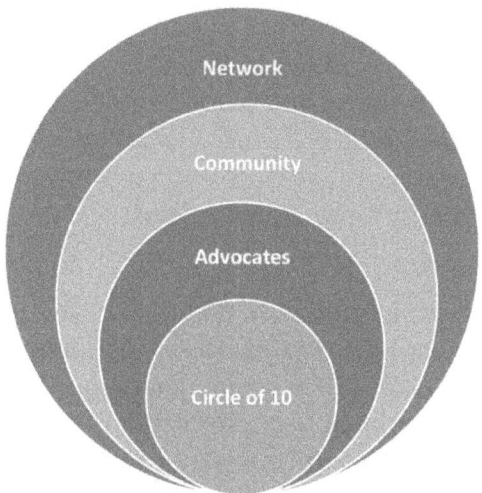

Examples of social capital circles:

The Circle of Ten (or the Circle of Friends): These are the people closest to you, who support, encourage, and inspire you. They are the people who are your champions. You can call people in this circle in the middle of the night and count on them to be there for you. They are the people you can trust most to be in your corner and support you. As you build a new business or strike out on a new venture or fall flat on your face, these are the people you can depend on to encourage, inspire, and motivate you to believe in yourself and to stay in the game.

Most people that I have coached have one or two Circle of Ten members when we start the process of developing a Circle of Ten. Seldom does anyone have more than three people in their circle. It takes an intentional course of action to develop your Circle of Ten. One of the questions I ask people is, "Are you willing to be a Circle of Ten person for someone else? If the answer is yes, you are ready to establish your own Circle of Ten. The first step is to develop a list of criteria for your Circle of Ten."

The second circle is your Advocate Circle. Advocates are essential in building valuable social capital and building and expanding your group coaching business. An advocate is someone who supports you and is willing to speak up on your behalf. Advocates are people who know you on a professional level and are so confident in your professionalism and ability that they will help you achieve the results you want. As you build social capital, you will become an advocate for many in your circles of connection, and as a result, you will develop advocates for you and your coaching groups.

Characteristics of an advocate
- Knows who you are and what you do.
- Acknowledges you as an accomplished professional in your field.
- Has a personal or professional relationship with you either now or in the past.
- Refers others to you on a regular basis.

As you mindmapp for advocates, you will include all your affiliations and connections with companies, organizations, associations, volunteer groups, and alliances. From each of those connections, you will identify one, two, or three advocates who know you and the contributions you have made in that group. One of the participants in a 12 Keys group recently told his group that he had a few "dis-advocates" in companies where he had worked. I replied, "Don't we all!" We all laughed heartily as he gave us permission to acknowledge our humanity. The key to this exercise is that we ignore our dis-advocates and focus on our advocates.

It is often startling for coaches as they go through the mindmapping process to discover how many people they know. This is easily visible on Facebook or LinkedIn. Connecting and reconnecting with colleagues, coworkers, members of professional groups, alumnae, friends, and relatives provide collaborating opportunities and can yield valuable advocates.

Coaching Skills and Tools: Mindmapping for Social Capital

Examples of mindmapping spokes that are centers of connection for many people:
- Companies/Corporations
- Organizations
- Businesses
- Community groups
- Circle of friends
- Collegial associations
- Industry associations
- Clients, both present or former
- Customers
- Prospects
- Students

According to Dr. Baker, the outcome of developing and growing rich social capital is that you can become a linchpin. Linchpins are those people who "provide the shortcuts that convert a big world into a small one." They are the people who bridge gaps and connect divergent groups of people into a network. Linchpins are typically generous people who spread ideas, information, and resources across many boundaries.

In Christie Kinsey's linchpin example below, please look for the ways in which Christie was able to build her social capital and the effect that it had on her professionally and personally.

Group Coaching Example

Christie Kinsey, a financial representative with Northwestern Mutual Financial Network, is a favorite example of becoming a linchpin in her community. She has an extensive entrepreneurial network that has been achieved by her intention to make a contribution to others in her life and in her community.

Christie started her career as a teller in a local bank in the town of Huntington, West Virginia, where she grew up. When she became a Northwestern financial representative over twenty-five years ago, she built her business as she actively participated in her community. Her intention was to give generously to others without expecting anything in return but with the confidence that her business would grow as she grew as a business professional who held true to her business ethics and values to place the best interest of her clients first.

In the twenty-five years since, Christie has served her community generously and effectively. As president of the Huntington Museum of Art, she encouraged the development of programs that involved more people in museum activities, including large numbers of children. As a result, the museum's outstanding children's program received national recognition and a community grant from Northwestern Mutual. She also served for several years on the Huntington Hospital board of directors and recently as chairman of that board. She is a founding member of a women's political action committee and a member of a philanthropy group. She readily volunteered as a mentor in her financial services company in a group coaching project where I was the coach. She was able to model social capital development with the members in the coaching group, and as a result, several of the members of that group have developed rich and valuable social capital and flourished in their business as a result of having both a mentor and a coach.

Social Capital Model

Social capital is often developed in a three-tiered model.

Level One: Networking

The networking activity level is the foundation of your social capital. It involves identifying your ideal clients, showing up where they work and connect, and intentionally establishing relationships with those potential clients and advocates. You can be successful by staying on this level by following through consistently, by giving referrals and support, and by receiving referrals from others.

The only drawback in not going to the other levels is that after fifteen years in the business, you are still at this level, feeling like you are constantly marketing and prospecting for business. The rewards may be good financially and you may attract some successful clients, but it can feel like you are starting over every year.

Level Two: Creating Advocates

Spheres of influence, board of directors, angels, champions, or advocates are some of the names you may call those wonderfully collaborative people with whom you have meaningful human moments and who help you build your business as you help them build their business or advance in their organizations. You are creating a community of support and care by turning your contacts into advocates.

Staying in touch with your advocates and adding new ones all the time is your mission at this level while taking advantage of those opportunities to give and receive.

Level Three: The Linchpin Level

Linchpins spread ideas, information, and resources. They are the gateways between many different groups of people and are the go-to people who help you find a great realtor, secure financing for your latest project, get a bond issue passed for a new school, provide expertise in a field so you can tap their brain, help you find a new employee, provide you with an opportunity to help others, or give you a chance to grow and learn your next step.

A successful financial services professional I coached for several years has been implementing the social capital model continually, and he just had his best year ever despite the economy. He is really getting that this is making prospecting so much easier and more fun. He didn't realize how big his horizons could be.

After he had been staying on track with Level One, he quickly increased it a notch. As he clarified and upgraded his client base, he improved his listening and communication skills so that he focused on long-term relationships with all his clients.

He systematically made appointments with those people he admired, respected, and those who make a difference in his community. He learned to connect with his ideal clients regularly by asking about their businesses so he could learn about their plans, visions, and dreams. He let all his advocates know what the focus was for his business and set up a board of directors to help him receive valuable feedback on his own business development. He created fair trade relationships where he supported others in building their business while asking those clients to help him grow his business. These new advocates were instrumental in his successful business growth. He set up meetings with advocates on his calendar for every single week he is in the office. Besides already reaping business benefits, he enjoys the process of giving and receiving with his new advocates.

The linchpin level has been a revelation for him. He had never thought of becoming a linchpin! He is suddenly thinking of how he can make a really powerful impact, be of great value to the community, and really move to a whole new level in his business. At the linchpin level, he is becoming the host of a community where people look to him for connections with people and organizations where they can grow and expand in a supportive environment.

What he has done so far:

He has sponsored an evening with the local children's theater, where the organization provided the entertainment, served wine and cheese, and welcomed him and fifty of his clients and friends. He discovered it was amazingly affordable and hosted a wonderful evening. The event provided welcome funding for the theater; a great experience for his advocates, clients, and friends; and he and his wife, Ann, had a great time.

Secondly, he joined the Economic Development Commission. He had considered it earlier, but once he joined he realized what an amazing opportunity it would be for him to give back to his city, help the overall economic growth of the area, and interact with the top business owners and professionals in the community.

He also is writing a quarterly financial column in the local newspaper. One of these columns was about a long-term care policy he wrote that allowed one of his customers to take care of her husband when he was diagnosed with ALS. The local paper came out and interviewed him along with the wife of his client about the value of long-term care insurance and how it made all the difference for the family through this difficult ordeal.

He also sponsored a hole at the local golf tournament at their small country club. He plans to have the company logo and his info on the flag at the hole and in all the sponsor pages for the tournament. He is delegating more and more of his buffer work and is having a lot more fun doing the level two and three areas of building social capital. He is rapidly becoming a linchpin in his community.

Case Study: "How I built *Choice* magazine through social capital and media."

A great social capital success story is that of my good friend, Garry Schleifer, publisher of *Choice* magazine (www.choice-online.com).

One of the first things to know about *Choice*, the magazine of professional coaching, is that it was created out of a vacuum. Being an entrepreneur I tend to see opportunities, and I realized in 2002 that the coaching profession did not have a magazine. After nine months of creative effort we launched the magazine in November 2003 at the International Coach Federation (ICF) International Conference in Denver.

Our initial and traditional community building was created by our personal attendance at the annual international conferences and having a booth where coaches could buy the first edition of the magazine and subscribe.

Remember that this is a "high touch" community, so personal response is extremely important. Not necessarily face-to-face, but most certainly person-to-person, coach-to-coach, friend-to-friend.

The continued growth of our community has been the result of being present wherever and whenever our target markets, primarily life coaches, were gathered. This meant attendance at local and regional conferences and monthly online meetings, all of which continued to grow our community.

Not long after the launch, we created an automated affiliate program so that our growing fan base could support us and they could make some passive revenue! Over the years we have connected with chapters and schools to send them sample issues of the magazine, including marketing materials to help and support them.

Another way we grow our community is by allowing non-subscribers to join our mailing list so they can benefit from the content we create and distribute. This allows us to capture even the passive visitor, those who "dip their toes" into our site. We continue to market to them with our paid and free offerings. We feel that the people who came on board this way have taken part, to a large extent, in revenue-generating opportunities, such as teleclasses and subscription offers.

In the new era of social media, we have added our presence as individuals and groups with LinkedIn, Facebook, and Twitter.

With the help of a social media coach, we are learning to rapidly grow, leverage, and use our social media community by adding value and suggesting opportunities both from us and from others who are supportive of the coaching profession and the overall success of coaches.

So this is all of the mechanics of the creation of a social network. What may not be evident is that all of this was done based on a personal need and design to collaborate and bring a value of generosity. The saying, "If I can help others get what they want, I will get what I want" is imprinted on my brain. Sometimes it's been too much, as can be seen in our early days of giving too much at times.

Besides teleclasses led by top professionals in the coaching arena, we also provide opportunities for coaches to be mentored by coaches in the network and invite people to join coaching groups within the *Choice* network. The *Choice* fan base continues to grow.

Garry Schleifer, PCC
Concept Synoptic Inc.
Publisher of *Choice* magazine
garry@conceptsynoptic.com
www.choice-online.com
www.conceptsynoptic.com

Coaching Questions
1. Who have you identified as part of your circle of ten?
2. How many companies, organizations, and associates are you a member of now or have you been a member of in the past?
3. Do you keep in contact with your advocates on a regular basis? Calls, lunches, meetings, social events?
4. Are you actively connecting in social networks online?
5. Do you keep your contact database up-to-date?
6. Are you becoming a linchpin in your community?

Chapter Four
Confidential Connections

"For it is mutual trust, even more than mutual interest that holds human associations together."
H. L. Mencken US editor (1880-1956)

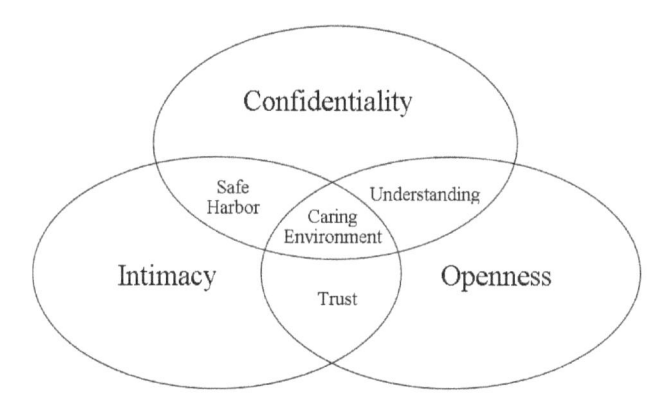

Creating Confidentiality and Trust in the group

Several years ago, Candace, a financial services group member, shared her dilemma in her coaching group. Her mother in a nearby city was in the last stages of breast cancer, her husband and son needed more of her time and attention, and her growing business was dependent on her daily leadership. Her added anguish over the lack of help and support that her siblings were giving her in managing her mother's care was evident to all the coaching group members.

At my invitation and with Candace's permission, the group did a round-robin, an opportunity for each of them to support her, encourage her, and brainstorm with her for possibilities. As her coach, I was able to see an opportunity to step in and ask her about her own self-care and to encourage her to explore how she might expand her opportunities to ask for the help she needed.

At the end of our call, she tearfully expressed her gratitude to be able to share honestly with others without censoring her circumstances. She was especially appreciative to have a support team in place during this time. It was the confidentiality and trust that the group had built during the two years together that allowed her to share fully. Throughout the following months, her group challenged and encouraged her to delegate and reach out to others for support and help.

A year later, she shared with her group how she had delegated more to her office staff and how they had stepped up brilliantly to the challenge. She also explained how she had reached out to her brother for very specific help and how he had responded favorably to her request. Everyone in the family had always accepted that Candace could handle anything and, therefore, had assumed she didn't need help. She was especially excited that after requesting help from her husband and son that they had stepped up to share her load at home. She proudly shared how grateful she was to have been there for her mother in those final months. In an especially emotional moment, Candace announced that she had participated in a breast cancer three-day walk to raise funds and awareness for the disease, and her mom had been there at the finish line, knowing Candace had dedicated the walk to her. These conversations happened in the context of a professional coaching group in a major financial services company as part of an initiative to recruit, retain, and increase the production of top women producers in the organization. Candace said a large part of her success in navigating through this difficult time was the opportunity to share her story honestly and fully within the group and having the support, encouragement, and resources provided by her group and her coach.

As a result, she was able to collect some great ideas, have the courage to ask for help at work and at home, make a shift in her thinking about taking good care of herself during that difficult time, and recognize that her coaching group was more than a professional group, that these were advocates that she could count on throughout the most difficult time of her life.

During that year, she maintained her production level without losing any business, created closer family relationships, and gained new energy and confidence personally and professionally.

An environment of openness, confidentiality, and trust was essential in order for her to share her story and her life circumstance with the other professionals in her group.

To develop trust and confidentiality, I have developed certain criteria in the coaching model that facilitate openness and honesty.

INDEPENDENCE

Group members don't share the same offices, employees, direct reports, or team members. The group members are often affiliated with the same company or organization, but they do not share the same office location or staff. They may be focused on achieving an industry standard or goal or have a desire for developing and growing their entrepreneurial businesses, or they may have the same personal or professional obstacles or opportunities, but they are not working together on a regular basis.

1. **CHOICE**

   The members choose to be a part of the group coaching program or initiative offered by their company. Organizations in collaboration with a coach often make the decision on the overall mission and focus of the group, and the company makes the program available to those who qualify or are deemed appropriate for the group. Once an invitation to join the group is sent to potential members, they can choose whether or not to join the program.

2. **CONFIDENTIALITY**

   Members who join the group are asked to make a pledge of confidentiality. That pledge is a written one and involves a commitment to not sharing audio recordings as well as personal observations about others. I often say, "Share anything you personally said or anything you experienced in the group meeting, just don't share what others say or experience."

3. **TRANSPARENCY**

   If you are working with a company or organization, it is important to have clear agreements about transparency and confidentiality by setting up independent audio and conferencing systems so that they are not a part of the company conferencing systems. That way the group knows the recordings won't be shared with others internally. Also, it is essential to have an agreement that the coach will share nothing with management without the knowledge of and agreement of the member or members involved. Having complete transparency with the participants in the group gives them the confidence to share openly. A group member must agree on what information will be shared and typically is involved in any conversation between the coach and management.

4. **STANDARDS**

    Creating a coaching environment requires that members agree to consistent standards. That agreement may include honoring each other's privacy, confidentiality, choices, expertise, and contributions. Instead of giving advice to others, group members learn to coach each other by asking curious and important questions, listening very carefully, reflecting, challenging, supporting, and most of all championing each other.

The International Coach Federation Code of Ethics is an excellent document that merits regular review. In establishing coaching agreements, the coach can refer to this document in the process of educating organizations and individual clients on the ethical standards of credentialed coaches. That makes the standards of confidentiality clear from the onset of the coaching relationship and adds credibility.

Creating a Confidential Environment

As you meet the first time to launch the group, there are some tools for creating trust and connection.

- Discuss the group guidelines and what they mean to each group member individually and demonstrate and practice those guidelines consistently in the group environment.
- Brainstorm ways this group can create an environment grounded in trust and confidentiality. As their coach, it is important to acknowledge and explore all suggestions.
- To encourage connection between members quickly, you can ask one or more powerful questions that evoke responses that highlight feelings, rather than intellectualizing and storytelling. Example: What is it that you bring to your peers that will be incredibly valuable to the other group members?

Examples of other powerful questions that may help individuals connect with and appreciate their fellow group members are:

- On a really good day, when everything is going great, what do you enjoy most about your profession?

- What is something that you enjoy doing so much that you lose track of time and place when you're doing it?
- What is one thing that you can always count on in your life or in your business?

The Evolution from an Unformed Group to a Formed Group

If the group hasn't been together long, and if individuals in the group don't know each other, then it is an unformed group. One of the first intentions of a group coach is to move the group from an unformed to a formed group so group members can own their own group. Below are the distinctions and some tools and ideas for doing that.

Unformed Group	Formed Group
Personally focused	Centered outward
Not engaging with others	Interacting with others
Phoning, texting	Questioning, sharing
Slow to step up to coaching	Moves quickly into coaching
Creating their own agenda	Co-creating a group agenda
Single focus ("I" oriented)	Shared focus ("We" oriented)

Designing environments as a group coach

By learning to design environments that bring the individuals in a group together quickly and create connections, coaches can help groups transition from unformed to formed groups easily.

In a formed group that has established confidentiality and trust, group members feel free to share honestly with the assurance that they will be heard fully and supported and validated by their coach and group.

In such a group, the communication is interactive and the group looks for value from group members as well as the coach. In that environment, honesty prevails so that challenges and messages can be delivered and received freely.

Often group members will say this is the only place I can count on people telling me the truth.

In a recent conversation with Philip Brew, a UK coach who serves on the ICF board of directors, we discussed the differences between a facilitated group and a coaching group. We both agreed that there was one concept that was truly the distinguishing difference, and that concept was ownership. If the group has the ownership of the group rather than the coach, then it truly qualifies as a coaching group.

Some characteristics of formed groups

- Formed group members share a firm belief in the reliability of the group and the group members.
- Formed group members honor, respect, and value each other's privacy and choices.
- Each coaching group environment is a space intentionally designed so that members connect and develop relationships by participating and sharing generously.
- Extraordinary results are common in a group environment built around confidentiality and trust.
- The environment requires that all members be fully present with their group so they can listen actively and take cues to share from each other.

Coaching tools for forming and connecting a group

- Group members are given the opportunity to participate freely.
- Group members co-create the group design and focus.
- Invitations to collaborate are part of every communication with group members.
- Participants feel comfortable agreeing or disagreeing.
- Members accept or reject invitations without feeling uncomfortable or judged.
- Participants have a choice stay more involved and committed.

Example of a formed group exchange

The following are e-mail communications exchanged in a formed group in a large financial services company that hired me to help retain top female financial representatives. This was a formed group, who had been together over two years, and one of the members, Suzanne, had missed two meetings in the course of three months without sharing a reason or explanation.

A few members of her group were very upset with her and stepped up to express their displeasure. The result of this exchange was that her peers challenged her and stood up for themselves, each other, and their group. It was only after her apology and recommitment to the group that Suzanne was forgiven and, after being given a second chance, stepped up and showed up for the group meetings. As a result, she became a more committed and integral part of the group, and the group was more cohesive and successful. The group didn't wait for the group coach to intervene or step into the decision. The group knew who owned their group, and they accepted Suzanne's apology and allowed her to continue based on the condition of regular attendance.

> Dear Suzanne,
> I get the feeling from your lack of being present that our group is not important enough to you to keep as a regular appointment. I, personally, do not have the patience for it. If you are not going to be there, I think you should be booted from the group.
> —Ann
>
> Hi Suzanne,
> You committed to a goal (like being on the calls) and didn't complete it. I took your request to Ginger to not get booted as the easy way out (no offense to Ginger, but she doesn't make that executive decision, we are the group). If actions speak louder than words, then why did you miss the meeting? I am personally in the midst of making some big decisions and need the full participation of our group. I would encourage you to live up to the commitment and be there.
> —Paula
>
> Hi Suzanne, you are forgiven—I love you!!! We just missed you. We had a good call, but it is never the same without you.
> Love, Cindy
>
> Dear Ginger, Cindy, Paula, Ann, Denise, and Marie,
> Please accept my apologies for missing our call yesterday, and I acknowledge I missed another meeting this quarter. The way I had it in my calendar wasn't clear because I had another appointment written right below it. I feel really stupid and will kindly request that the group not boot me out. I promise to not miss another meeting. Thank you for your patience with me.
> Love, Suzanne

Formed Group Standards
- Inclusion
- Attendance
- Brainstorming
- Creative design
- Active listening
- Co-creation of agendas
- Confidentiality
- Supporting and challenging peers
- Authenticity
- Accountability and responsibility
- Feedback from the coach and peers in the group
- Shared reactions
- Shared insight and awareness
- Deeper and more powerful questions
- Direct communication
- Unconditional respect

The intention of the group coach is to move the group as quickly as possible to a formed group so the group becomes interdependent. In a formed group, they become focused and receptive to the wisdom, insight, and value that their fellow group members bring to the call. Once they become a formed group, all the momentum, insight, action, accountability and connection that allow groups to grow and achieve results occurs. When the group is confident in their connection and create intimacy, they can collaborate and learn with each other and succeed at a high level.

Graduation Example from a Coaching Group

Several years ago, a group of corporate women who had been together in a coaching group for four years graduated. We had a virtual ceremony with awards, speeches, and a graduation party. Each woman expressed how coaching and the group had transformed her life. Susan said that coaching was no longer a tool or skill for her but had become a part of who she is and that now she experiences it on a "cellular level."

They all spoke about how their lives, their businesses, and their relationships had grown and flourished in the four years. They talked of how the group had provided a harbor for honesty, a comfort in times of difficulties, a reservoir of wisdom, a whine-free zone, a platform for accountability and responsibility and created a lasting circle of caring advocates for each of them. We shared gales of laughter and several tears.

Group Case Study: Dr. Zuno Kristal, Tel Aviv, Israel

A group member was exiled because he was not connecting and contributing. In group coaching, connection is a key factor in allowing the coaching process to work so the group members are making meaningful changes. You cannot change what you are not aware of. Connection also relates to the capacity of the client to be aware of the process itself, and that allows him or her to be committed to the process. In my experience, a group client needs to be aware of what is it that he or she wants to work on and then to be willing to make a commitment to the coaching process.

An added aspect when a client moves from individual coaching to group coaching is a willingness to make a commitment to the group. It is not only about one person's process, it is about the group process.

In one of the groups I was coaching, one member of the group was not participating as actively as the rest of his peers. This member was sitting quietly on the side in most of the meetings, and when others asked him his opinion or asked him a question, he answered that he wanted to learn by listening rather that sharing. Well, in group coaching, part of the process of being an active member of the group means being fully present and verbally sharing, not simply listening.

In this case, after a few weeks of meeting together, the group realized that this specific member had a different agenda than the rest of the group, and he was challenged to define his commitment to the group. Since he was very determined that his role was confined to being a listener only, the group asked him to leave. I find this example illustrates the relevance and high importance of awareness of one's role and commitment in the group coaching process and the power of a formed group to own the group and set standards and keep and enforce commitments.

Zuno Kristal, EdD
Kristal Coaching
zuno@kristalcoaching.com
www.kristalcoaching.com

Coaching Questions—Trust and Confidentiality
1. What are three characteristics that are shared by all group members?
2. What are the individual strengths that each member brings to the group?
3. Who is a natural connector in the group?
4. Can you as their coach step out of the way and let the group make natural connections and handle conflicts outside of the group meetings?
5. How do you see your role as you champion for each group member and for the group as a whole?

Chapter Five
Active Listening in a Coaching Group

"The most basic of all human needs is the need to understand and be understood. The best way to understand people is to listen to them."
—Ralph Nichols

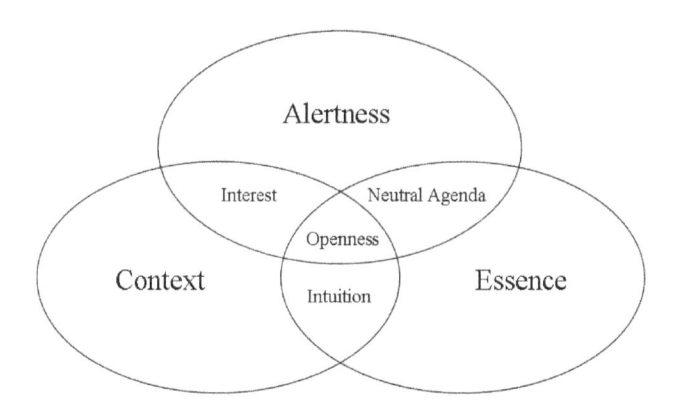

```
                    Alertness
            Interest    Neutral Agenda
                  Openness
      Context                    Essence
                  Intuition
```

Listening well is the key to being an effective coach and has very little to do with hearing. Hearing is purely based on auditory functions. When you listen, you engage all of your senses, including listening for tone, pitch, inflection as well as awareness of a person's body language.

Listening actively within a group requires that you not only listen to what is being said in the group, but also learn to focus intently on listening at a deeper level. Specifically, listening intentionally for clues and opportunities to discover what is deeper and more meaningful in what group members are saying. I love the fifteen "Listening Clarifiers" that Thomas J. Leonard developed as a tool for helping coaches listen for specific things that may be an opportunity for coaching (see below.)

Active listening is a core competency with the International Coach Federation and is defined as "The ability to focus completely on what the clients is saying and is not saying, to understand the meaning of what is said in the context of the client's desires, and to support client self-expression." By coaching groups, a coach accepts the challenge and an opportunity to become an expert in listening to others.

Here are some surprising statistics from the International Listening Association:

How much of what we know that we have learned by listening?	85%
Amount of the time we are distracted, preoccupied, or forgetful?	75%
How much do we recall immediately after we listen to someone?	50%
Amount of time we spend listening?	45%
How much we remember of what we hear?	20%
Those who have had formal educational training in listening	2%

As you are coaching groups, your active listening will be escalated to a higher level in order for you as the coach to listen to all the individuals in the group, to listen for what is missing from the conversation, to listen for what is next for the group conversation, and to listen for the opportunities to take the conversation to a richer, deeper level. Thomas Leonard coined the phrase "tri-plex" listening to describe what occurs when coaches are listening on multiple levels. The focus is more than what is being said; it's about the intention of the group members, which can include who is speaking and what they're saying, who is responding and who is missing from the conversation.

Active listening is also about being comfortable with silence. It is so tempting to step into that silent space, when it is it appropriate and enlightening to say nothing.

I love this analogy that one of the 12 Keys Mentoring Group shared.

> The analogy I use is that individual coaching is a bit like tapping your foot and rubbing your tummy. And group coaching is like tapping your foot, rubbing your tummy, clicking your fingers, and patting your head. So, you have to get the coaching process right. And then you have to manage the other layers of what you are doing such as the group dynamics, being aware of who is a passive listener (which is all right because that's how they get on), and who is not participating (which is not working and there is something there that you have to address). So, what has become patently obvious is that group coaching is a layer on top of coaching skills.

Peter Rowe
ProfiTune Business Systems
www.profitune.com

Guidelines to Elevate Listening Skills

There are some important guidelines to elevate listening skills in a group:

Listen twice as much as you talk in the group

When a coach says more than seven sentences in a row, it becomes a monologue rather than a dialogue. The rules of engagement in a coaching group necessitate listening and then questioning to ensure everyone is part of the conversation. Coaches starting groups for the first time seem to naturally focus on sharing the content and expertise that they can bring to the coaching group rather than encouraging group members to share their expertise and wisdom.

Just as the role of a coach with an individual client is to listen carefully and stay on the client's agenda by asking powerful questions that evoke the information needed to help that client move forward on their journey, the role of a group coach is to listen carefully to the group as a whole and to the individual participants. Actively listening by the coach can uncover what is true in the present and collect the information necessary to facilitate future pathways and opportunities for the group.

Install laser speak guidelines

Allowing the opportunity for everyone to be fully listened to in group meetings is important to bonding and connecting the group. One of the best ways to do this is by setting an appropriate guideline that limits long detail-oriented stories that focus on in-depth explanations. By encouraging group members to get their information or focus out there quickly, the coach encourages the flow of ideas, feelings, and expressions around an issue to emerge so that coaching, encouraging, advising, and mentoring can take place. If laser speaking becomes the standard in the group, the coach won't have to monitor and challenge group members; the members themselves will be reminding each other.

Avoid interrupting

Give group members the opportunity to express themselves without interruption. If this becomes a standard in the group along with laser speaking, every member will be able to participate often and without concern that they will be interrupted or misunderstood. Reminders of both laser speak and no interrupting are important for the first few meetings of the group in order to establish these standards. All reminders should be general ones about honoring the guidelines rather than calling out individuals.

Stay charge neutral

An effective group coach operates best by not supporting or opposing group members' ideas or contributions, but remaining in the role of questioning and clarifying. One of the tools that is effective in doing that is remaining "charge neutral." Charge neutral is "no energy up" and "no energy down" when communicating or asking questions. This allows group members to respond and not react by promoting or defending what they have said.

If charge neutral becomes the coach's standard in the group, the environment created allows everyone to feel safe to express themselves without causing a reaction from their coach or creating a circumstance where they will be judged or criticized.

Ask clarifying questions and listen for the answers

By avoiding probing or leading questions, the coach creates an environment of curiosity and discovery. That environment provides the opportunity for creativity and excitement in the group. In identifying whether the group client is sharing an opportunity or simply a possibility allows the coach to coach that person more effectively and to prioritize agenda items within the group format.

Remain assumption free

One of the four agreements from Don Miguel Ruiz in his best seller, *The Four Agreements*, is "Don't make assumptions." What a great reminder to a coach leading a group to listen for clarification, for context, for feedback, for perceptions, and for understanding. This requires that you be fully present as a coach and not focused on your own agenda for the group. One of the exercises I encourage group members to do is to spend twenty-one days being assumption free. Quite a challenge and yet attainable if the participants ask a question every time they are tempted to make an assumption.

Identify the opportunity for specific member input

By identifying individual group members' strengths and expertise, the coach can open opportunities to highlight group members and allow group wisdom to emerge. The key here is that a coaching group is a peer group where every member is an expert at something. By collaborating and sharing wisdom with their fellow group members, rich and valuable resources are shared. I ask groups at the end of each meeting to tell us what they have found valuable in our time together. Most often group members share what another member said that enlightened them, challenged them, informed them, or inspired them. It is important for coaches not to want or need to be the focus of value in the group, but to recognize that more often than not, it is their peers who provide the most insight and value.

It is also important to listen for group members' feelings. By letting that person know you hear and understand his or her feelings, everyone feels safe to share. It is also important to be the coach for the group as well as for the individual. When a member's circumstance is not relevant or appropriate for the entire group, the coach can suggest having an individual laser coaching conversation outside the group to deal with a particular concern or opportunity. Having that option is valuable to the client and can allow the group to move forward comfortably.

Tool for Listening Actively

Thomas J. Leonard created the listening clarifiers for coaches to raise the listening bar. The fifteen clarifiers provide a valuable framework for listening actively.

1. **Urgent or Important**
   Is the matter urgent or merely important?
   Example Question: What is the long-term impact of inaction?

2. **Addressed or Avoiding**
   Is the client addressing a problem or situation or avoiding it?
   Example question: What are the consequences of avoiding this problem for your business or your life?

3. **Accurate or Interpretation**
   Is the client being accurate or are they interpreting?
   Example question: As your coach, I want to be sure I am correct in my interpretation of what you just said.

4. **Open or Resistant**
   Does the client sound open or resistant about what they are sharing with their coach and the group?
   Example question: Are you open to having a conversation about this now?

5. **Internal or External Reference Point**
   Is what the client saying coming from them or from an external reference point?
   Example: Is this your goal or dream or is it someone else's dream?

6. **Want or Could/Should/Need**
   Is it a want or a something very different?
   Example: How might you identify if this is something you need to do or something you really want to do?

7. **Opportunity or Possibility**
   Is it a real opportunity or just a possibility?
   Example question: Is this something that you daydream about doing one day or something that they want to achieve now?

8. **Source or Symptom**
   Is it the source of the problem or a symptom?
   Example question: Do you remember when this was first a concern for you?

9. **Opening or Share**
   Is what the client saying an opening for change or just an opportunity to share? Resistance?
   Example: Is this an area where you want to make a change immediately?

10. **Response or Reaction**
    Is the client responding to a situation or reacting to it? Relevance?
    Example: What are you feeling about this situation today?

11. **Create or Eliminate**
    Is the client creating something or reducing or eliminating something? Timing?
    Example question: Are you tolerating something that needs to be eliminated immediately?

12. **Problem or Concern**
    Is the client presenting a problem or just a concern? Speaks to relevance?

Example question: On a scale of one to ten, how important is this to you at this moment?

13. **Present or Past**

    Is the client coming from the present or the past? Effect on moving forward?

    Example: Is this something you want to move forward on immediately?

14. **Acceptance or Resistance**

    Is the client accepting a change or new reality or resisting it? Difference in energy?

    Example question: How are you feeling about accepting this new position?

15. **Toward or Away From**

    Is the client moving toward something or away from something? Timing?

    Example: When will you be comfortable about making a decision?

Active listening has many benefits, including:
- Being heard engenders trust and intimacy in group participants.
- When a group member is listened to confidentially, it creates an environment of safety.
- Listening improves the opportunity for change, new ideas, and innovation.
- Feeling heard and understood raises member participation in coaching groups.
- Assuring client engagement and satisfaction.
- Reducing assumptions and creating clarity for the member and the group.
- Builds rapport and connection with the peers in the group.
- Demonstrates support and involvement of group members.

The truth about listening as a coach:
- Your intention and focus determine how well you listen. Your listening needs to be tailored to the person with whom you are talking.
- Open your ears to hear everything being said so that you won't step over anything in your questions or responses.
- Being "out of judgment" provides you with a clean slate to hear, while getting rid of the chattering in your head.
- A person will tell you everything you need to know, including a plausible solution, if you actively listen.
- To be effective you must move away from your own thoughts and connect with the other person by listening.

Listen to what people are NOT saying as well as what they are saying
- Be comfortable with silence—recognize that you don't have to fill it with questions or comments.
- Hear what is not being said about their commitments and actions.
- Listen for changes in the client's focus and direction.
- Filter your listening to catch and eliminate personal judgments.
- Do not interrupt.
- Pause after a powerful question to allow the member to ruminate before responding.
- Listen for nonverbal cues such as hesitations, pen tapping, background noise, and an indication that a member has disappeared from the conversation.
- Filter through a member's sharing to find the kernel of insight and truth.
- Check in to make sure what you are hearing is what they are saying.
- Avoid jargon or coaching terms when asking someone to clarify a point.

Listening and Questioning for Clarification Example

As a young person I played the cello and enjoyed it very much. I shared this within a coaching group several years ago—a group where I was a member and not the coach. I told them how much I missed playing and wondered if I should resume practicing with the intention of playing in an orchestra again. The group was very supportive and enthusiastic in encouraging me to go back to my cello. The coach of the group didn't join in the encouragement, but was listening carefully and began asking me questions.

He asked me to share with the group what I enjoyed most about playing the cello. After thinking a few minutes, I shared that my mother was a fine pianist who would practice with me. I beamed as I told the group how wonderful it was to be with her and have her set the tempo and encourage me as I played. Then the coach asked me, "Will you enjoy the experience of practicing the cello by yourself?" Suddenly, I realized it was not so much my cello I missed, but the love of creating music with my mother. I had a flash of certainty that I would not want to practice the cello alone at all even if I played and practiced part of the time with a group. It was an "aha" moment for me. Now I listen to more music featuring cellos and think often about my musical experiences with my mother, but I don't long to play the cello myself. What insight and clarity came from the coach's active listening and powerful questioning.

Group Coaching Example

Being an active listener is like being a detective developing leads. One of the members of an entrepreneurial business owners coaching group had identified a coaching developmental skill he wanted to address. The skill he wanted to improve was to become a better listener. As the owner of a chain of sports shops, he managed many people and was constantly on the go. He also was married and had three small children. He explained to me that when he was at home he was in angst because he felt like he needed to be at his business, and when he was at work he lamented that he didn't spend enough time with his sons. And at either place, he wasn't fully present and really listening.

He said the one bright spot was that he had breakfast each morning with his three sons. I asked if they were comfortable sharing their experiences and ideas with him. He said that actually he had the television on, catching up with the business news of the day, while eating with them. I asked him if he was really having breakfast with his sons. He hesitated a moment and then recognized and acknowledged he was only sitting at the table with them and not listening at all. After an inventory of his days, he discovered that he was not really listening very well to those around him anywhere. The first action he took was turning off the television and listening to his sons every morning. From this first step he expanded the opportunities to listen throughout his day. He turned off his phone and his text messaging while having conversations during his day.

By cutting out distractions and being fully present with those around him, he started implementing his new listening skills. Playing that detective role was a great metaphor for him to start collecting clues and information from others. He was now listening actively and feeling more connected both at his businesses and at home. His focus on listening alerted him of the opportunities he had to become a better parent and boss. It also has made him a better group member and a happier person.

Group Coaching Listening Case Study

Active Listening—Teresa Pool, PCC, CPBA

I am frequently asked to coach leadership teams that struggle with collaboration. These dynamic leaders excel at managing their own silo of responsibility but often fail to "listen actively" to the impact of their peer's organizations when creating and executing their own plans. This results in a lack of cohesive strategy across the company or division and poor relationships among the leaders, which trickles down through their departments. Rather than seeing their peers as partners, they are viewed as barriers to get around.

To address this challenge and reboot the team relationship, we bring the leaders together for an exercise in active listening.

I begin by facilitating a high-level discussion about the goals, achievements, and challenges in the division. This gets all the leaders back into the big picture mind-set of what they are working toward as a whole.

We bring the existing silo approach, the "elephant in the room," out for an active discussion. Everyone is asked to share, uninterrupted, how the lack of collaboration and cooperation is affecting their ability to meet their department goals and the division goals. This can be a lively discussion that requires strong facilitation skills to allow everyone to be heard without escalating into conflict.

Then each leader completes an exercise where they write down:
1. How they contribute to this silo challenge.
2. One collaborative strength of each peer.
3. How they believe each peer contributes to the silo challenge.
4. What one change they would like see from each peer.
5. Next, each leader takes a turn in the "active listening" seat.
6. The leader begins by sharing how they believe they contribute to the challenge.

7. Then each of their peers and the senior leader take turns sharing collaborative strengths, how they believe the leader contributes to the silo challenge, and what change they would like to see.
8. The leader "listens actively," without rebuttal, to each input then rephrases back what they have heard and asks for clarification.
9. The leader writes down all of the feedback and desired changes onto what becomes their collaboration scorecard.

Once all the feedback has been given and received, each leader reviews their scorecard and selects the changes to which they are willing to commit. We go around the table once more to hear from each leader what they have discovered from this "active listening" exercise and the changes they will make.

We close with how we will hold accountability to the committed changes and revisit what the division and results will look like when all the commitments are met. A follow-up session is usually held within ninety days.

This active listening exercise has been described as both painful and powerful, both good catalysts for change!

Teresa Pool, PCC, CPBA
President, Transitions for Business
teresa@transitionsforbusiness.com
www.transitionsforbusiness.com
Subscribe to the Transitions newsletter *The Peak Performer*

Coaching Questions:
1. Are you listening for coaching opportunities with your group clients and not just passively listening to them as they interact?
2. Are your coaching groups having dialogues in which everyone actively participates?
3. Do your group members enforce the laser-speaking standards in their groups so the groups are not exchanging monologues?
4. Are you aware when someone is missing from the group conversation?
5. Are you listening without making any assumptions and asking questions for clarity?
6. Are you listening three times as much as you are speaking in a group coaching meeting?

Chapter Six
Laser Speaking—
Everyone in the Conversation

"The less you talk, the more you are listened to."
—Abigail Van Buren, advice columnist

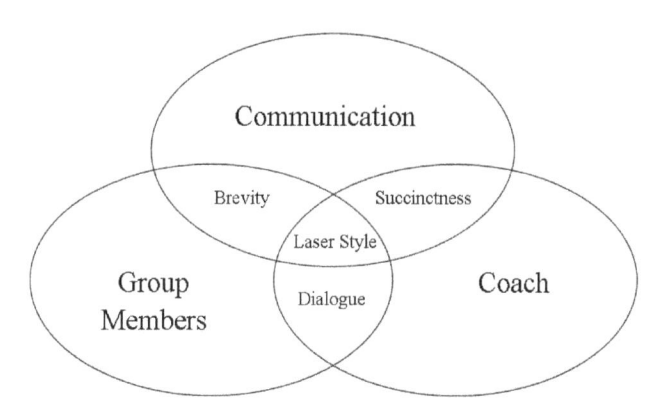

[Venn diagram with three overlapping ovals labeled "Communication", "Group Members", and "Coach". Overlap regions labeled: Brevity, Succinctness, Laser Style, Dialogue.]

Laser Speak—Everyone in the Conversation

One of the standards for every group I coach is the coaching skill of laser speak. Laser speak is an effective method for zeroing in on the core or the heart of ideas, concepts, information, and experiences that individuals share with others. It is about encouraging group members to convey their thoughts in the fewest words possible in the shortest time so that everyone is an integral part of the conversation. When laser speak is happening there is an energetic exchange of ideas. We define laser speak as the succinct, specific, and efficient use of words that gets to the heart of the matter.

The benefits of laser speak include maximizing group time together, minimizing unproductive bantering, encouraging more individual participation, creating time spaces for sharing important ideas and issues, and preventing one or two persons from dominating the group interaction.

Laser speak also encourages group members to be fully present in order to speak and listen to ideas being exchanged so briefly and to the point because otherwise they might miss something important. A group member will often ask that group members eliminate all distractions around them because there is noise on the line, and he or she doesn't want to miss anything on the call. For some members who are easily distracted, even a small diversion might prevent them from fully hearing everything or become sidetracked during the group call. A quiet environment also allows group members to be fully present and focused, and laser speak is much easier to practice.

Practicing laser speak also sharpens each individual's thinking because in order to laser speak, group members must process information effectively, filter out unnecessary commentary, and find the kernels of wisdom that are the heart of the matter.

Decision makers in companies often ask while we are in the negotiating phase of creating coaching groups how I know that people in the groups are not answering e-mails or playing computer games rather than taking part in the coaching group meeting. One of the keys to ensuring full group engagement is with laser speak. When ideas are exchanged quickly in the group, then it becomes obvious when someone is missing from that exchange. As the coach steps up to enroll that person back into the group conversation, then the entire coaching group learns to practice that skill. This ensures that no one is left behind in the group.

As a group coach, I keep a list of participant names on a side of the form I use with each group. That way I can put a check by each participant when they contribute during the call. If someone is not a participant in the discussion, it becomes obvious very quickly that they are missing in action, and that gives me the opportunity to check in with that person immediately for feedback. When they are all laser speaking frequently, it also confirms that the conversation is relevant and engaging for everyone on the call. When the energy in the group drops from lack of participation, it is time for the coach to check in with the group about whether it is time to wrap up on a topic and head in a new direction. A masterful group coach can feel that energy shift in a group quickly and check in with the group and ask about the relevancy and value of the current topic of conversation. Group members then have the opportunity to respond and step up with what works best for them.

A key indicator that the group interaction is going well is the energy level. One of the skills group coaches develop is an "energy barometer" to measure the energy level in the group. One coach, Ann, who coaches groups on location said that she has learned to tell when the energy starts to drop in the room, and she immediately addresses the environmental change and encourages questioning and laser speaking as a tool for regenerating a lackluster group. She will bring the group members together for a game or a feedback session, or use music or laughter to re-energize participants. The key piece is to re-engage the group as quickly as possible.

One of the best ways to make laser speak a standard in a group is to demonstrate it consistently by the coach. Initially, the coach will remind the group to practice it, and ultimately the group will monitor laser speak themselves. A quick reminder to a "long-winded" group member, "Don't forget to laser speak," is typically all it takes to stop the offender and move the group back to an interactive model for communicating. Once the group becomes formed and owns their group, the coach no longer plays that laser speak monitor and group members monitor themselves and their fellow group members. The value of energy and momentum on the call is so high that members become committed to maintaining laser speak within the group dynamics.

Specific Values of Laser Speaking in Group Coaching

Laser speak creates a richer learning environment as participants become more thoughtful and intentional about their contributions.

Laser Speak in Coaching Groups:
- Maximizes the time a group has together and minimizes time wasted.
- Encourages total participation by minimizing monopoly of one or two group members.
- Infuses the collective energy by keeping momentum in the communication.
- Helps the group maintain focus on the agenda items.
- Encourages clarity by leaving the space for group members to check in to clarify or question.
- Laser questions and laser comments build involvement and momentum.
- Allows for diversity of ideas because everyone has input in all the conversations.
- Requires participants to examine ideas for clarity as well as brevity.
- Keeps the energy level on the call high.

- Sharpens individual thinking when communication is brief and clear.
- Avoids group members "tuning out" because the calls become slow and boring.
- Encourages awareness and insight by allowing multiple points of view.
- Moves group members from discussion to action steps.

In order for a group coach to instill laser speak in a coaching group, it is important to start from the initial formation of a group to make it a part of the culture.

Coaching Tools and Skills for Implementing Laser Speak

Guidelines
Before group members meet the first time, they are sent a group coaching packet with guidelines for the group.

> **Example of Group Coaching Guidelines:**
> - Laser speak without story telling or long explanations. Get directly to the issue and the point.
> - Share your name before you speak in the group.
> - Be committed to achieving your own goals and helping others achieve theirs.
> - Stay focused on one issue at a time. Ask for group buy-in before changing the subject.
> - Hear out the member who has the floor before responding and then respond to add value.
> - Keep the feedback positive and encouraging.
> - Share whatever you wish about what you said in the meeting, not what anyone else said.
> - Please mute the call when you are in a noisy environment or may be interrupted.
> - Avoid advising unless requested. Coach people to discover their own answers.
> - Always ask permission before coaching or advising.
> - Bring your very best ideas and share them with the group.

Model laser speak as their coach
By consistently modeling laser speak, the group will quickly follow the model with the coach's occasional reminders and examples. When it is necessary to give a longer explanation or clarify a major point, it is important that the coach point out that this is departing from the norm and the reason for the change in the standard. It is then important to step back and re-establish laser speak as the standard.

Using Coach Prep Forms
Using coach preparation forms prior to meetings is an excellent way to distribute information among group members prior to the call. That way, specific situations and circumstances can be explained to group members by an exchange of e-mails so that when everyone joins the group, we can deal with the key components of a concern or opportunity and be able to question and laser speak.

Implementing co-created agendas
Implementing co-created agendas from the group prep forms gives rich opportunities for participants to make comments and choose options for meaningful agenda items. This allows everyone to be up to speed on agenda items before the group meeting. Also, as the coach, you can read e-mails from group members with agenda items ahead of time and look for key points to insure clarity and brevity.

Hear it, speak it, practice it
Two of the great teaching tenets for group learning are relevance and repetition, so make sure to point out examples of laser speak in the meetings and the value laser speak provides to group members. This encourages everyone to use laser speak.

Create additional places for non-laser speak
Examples of these alternative meetings are:
- **Adding an additional meeting per month** where they meet as a group without their coach. In that meeting, more detailed or in-depth discussions can take place.
- **Specific discussion forums** encouraging group members to meet with two or more members of the group to discuss a common interest. Example: Negotiation language for an exit strategy from a job or company.

- **Group buddies**, where connecting pairs of group members meet for opportunities to e-mail and talk in depth.
- "I wanted to stress the value of the emphasis on 'laser coaching' and Ginger's emphasis on helping members of the group practice laser speak. I had not heard that term before, but I have since used it to assist the groups I coach in communicating with each other without a lot of storytelling. Just succinct and specific language!" *Pat Walker, coach and consultant*

There are times when using laser speak in a group is not appropriate. It is important for the coach to recognize those times and acknowledge a special circumstance in the group and encourage more in-depth conversation. Some examples of this are:

1. Times of failure—when something isn't working or has failed miserably.
2. Times of extraordinary or unexpected success.
3. A relevant organization or business process change. Example: When companies implement new products or systems.
4. New ideas or opportunities that might affect all or most of the group members.
5. A new group member joining a group or a group member leaving a group.
6. Reinventing or reorganizing the group by the group members.
7. Brainstorming sessions for adjusting to a changing business environment.
8. A group member's personal crisis that is appropriate and important to share with their entire group. It is important for the coach to check with the group about this. They may wish to have the majority of the conversation in an individual session with the coach.

Laser Speak Exercise

A team member who presents an agenda item for the week invites another group member to listen to an update on their commitment for the week and to provide specific feedback. Here are some things that a listening partner should look for:

1. Was the update made in the allotted time?

2. How effective was the presenter in delivering the information in a clear and concise manner?
3. Note if any essential facts or information was missing or needed clarification.
4. How would you describe the presenter's ability to answer questions?

Laser Speak Example

As the owner of a property tax company where I was an agent representing property owners in negotiations with the local tax appraisal districts, I worked with three attorneys who had expertise in the industry. I found that by the time I had a meeting with them and explained all the details of the property I was representing, it was time consuming and expensive for me to use their services.

As a result I learned to identify the issue in a specific property fact scenario, so when I talked with one of the attorneys, I was able to laser speak, and they were quickly able to give me the point of law I needed on the phone. The goal was that I would give them the information they needed in no more than three sentences. The result was I got what I needed at a reduced cost and often at no charge at all. I learned quickly the value of laser speak.

Laser Speak Case Study—Holly O'Grady

I do a lot with laser speak, especially when I launch a group. One of the things that I really stress is how powerful laser speak is in business meetings. I have noticed that new hires in an organization do one of two things. They either stand apart from others in the meeting or they start constantly communicating for the purpose of fitting in and forming relationships (depending on their personality style).

If they withdraw, they can quickly become invisible and irrelevant in meetings and in the organization. The ones who are assertive and try to create conversations and relations can overdo it. As a result they are often too chatty and can start with these long preambles to quantify and qualify what they want to say. Often, by the time they get to the main point, no one is listening.

Learning to speak in a laser-like manner in a group setting—clearly and right to the point—gives them a lot of power. It's a good discipline, so we practice it a lot in e-group coaching so they can take that and apply when appropriate in the business setting. I think it gives them confidence, and it gives them a lot more impact and influence.

Holly A. O'Grady
Holly O'Grady Consulting
Action Learning Consultant at Partners for Learning and Leadership
holly.a.o'grady@aexp.com

> **Coaching Questions:**
> 1. Do you take the time to identify the issue or the key points with someone before you speak up in a group?
> 2. Do you edit and limit the words you use when you are participating in a group?
> 3. How do you feel when someone tells a long story reiterating the same points again and again?
> 4. What would be the advantage for you to improve your ability to laser speak?
> 5. Name three ways you could edit and upgrade your communication.

Chapter Seven

Powerful Questioning in a Group

"I never learn anything talking. I only learn things when I ask questions."
—Lou Holtz, US football coach

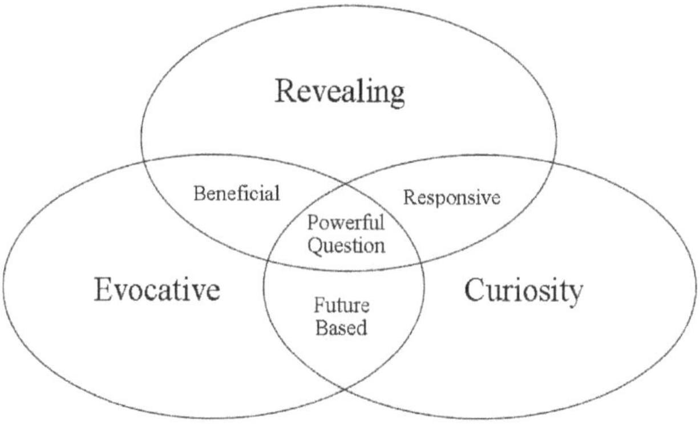

Revealing
Beneficial
Responsive
Powerful Question
Evocative
Curiosity
Future Based

The Wisdom Factor—engaging groups with powerful questions

"Wisdom is experience plus knowledge plus the power of application."

—Oxford American Dictionary

Experience + Knowledge + the Power of Application = WISDOM

Bringing peers together in a coaching group is a perfect environment for implementing the wisdom formula. Group members often find that the most value in a group meeting comes from shared wisdom within the group. This formula requires that there is a formed group with a coaching environment of confidentiality and trust along with a coach who is facilitating using the coaching competencies and proficiencies.

At a meeting in Dallas recently, a coach stopped me and said proudly that she had a group she had been coaching for eight months. I congratulated her and asked how the group was doing. She said with a sigh that she didn't know what to do next because she was running out of topics for the group, and she was constantly searching for new material. I asked if she had considered inviting the group members to bring their own agenda items and knowledge to the group. We sat down and had a conversation about how that might happen. I have coached groups that have thrived for as long as four years. Can you imagine as a coach having to bring new content to the group twice a month for four years?

Groups stay vital and relevant when the coach is only one of the contributors to the group, and the peer members in the group bring their agenda items to their coaching calls. In that scenario, a coach can supplement with ideas and resources, share other group members' ideas and personal experience and expertise, and encourage relevant presentations and contributions from contributors outside the group. In every reminder that we send out in advance of group meetings, I ask group members to share their agenda items and their relevant information.

Not only do coaches starting groups often believe that they are responsible for bringing most of the knowledge and information to coaching groups, but also it often never occurs to them that the group connects and learns best when everyone collaborates in creating what occurs in the group. In the beginning, group members may come to the group looking to the coach for most of the knowledge shared in the group. A group coach contributes most by getting out of the way and allowing the knowledge and wisdom to be shared by the group members and then stepping in to provide coaching skills and tools to the group.

Groups are reality experiences with "just in time" learning opportunities. I received an e-mail from a group member in a financial group who wanted to add a concern he had to the next meeting agenda. Jim had recently brought in a more experienced representative in a particular area of the business to do joint work with a client. Jim's client needed a specific financial product to fit into his overall financial planning, and Jim had very little experience with the product or the particular area of financial planning. As a result of bringing in this experienced professional, Jim was experiencing some problems in balancing his loyalty to his client and his ability to work with the joint work partner who had a specific agenda. Jim wanted some input and wisdom from his group. When I sent out the e-mail reminder of our group call along with some agendas for our next meeting, I realized quickly that this was a relevant topic that other group members might have advice to offer or questions about. The exchange of e-mails started the conversation, and they honed in on Jim's specific problem.

When Jim's agenda item came up in the group, I suggested we might do a round-robin, where everyone shared a key point, question, or wisdom nugget for Jim. They all agreed quickly because they all wanted to express their experiences and opinions. After that exercise, the conversation focused entirely on Jim's situation. After a ten-minute discussion, Jim said he could now move forward and make a decision on what he wanted to do. Then we had a conversation about how Jim's experience could be valuable for everyone in the group. The group members agreed they needed some guidelines around joint work with their clients. They agreed to create some criteria based on their values about putting their client's best interest first in any partnership with other professionals. It was an excellent exercise for all of them, and they each agreed to forward their criteria for doing joint work with colleagues to their peers before the next call. As a result of Jim's "just in time" agenda item, each group member received value that could impact their businesses for years to come.

One of the most valuable skills that a group coach can use to make sure wisdom is evoked in a coaching group is powerful questioning. Albert Einstein said, "The important thing is not to stop questioning. Curiosity has its own reason for existing. Never lose a holy curiosity."

Powerful questioning is the ability to ask questions that reveal the information needed for maximum benefit to the coaching relationship and the client (ICF core competency). A group coach must be fully present and actively listening on several levels in order to ask the questions necessary to take the conversations to a deeper more meaningful level.

I frequently kick off a coaching group with a question that encourages an answer from each individual, allowing others in the group to see more of who the person is rather than what they do and where they live. These powerful questions are designed to highlight *who* the group member is rather than what they do. I will ask, "On a really good day, what do you experience in your business?" Instead of giving a short bio or a brief introduction, group members hear their peers talk about the great things about their business or what is not working right now. They often express the enjoyment they have for what they do, how much they treasure the connections they have with their clients, and what means the most to them in their business and professional lives.

When Beth Lyons starts a group, she asks people to choose a color and introduce themselves as that color with a brief explanation about why they chose that color. For example, "My name is Bob and I am blue like the ocean, deep, cool, always in motion and connected to everything."

Or, "My name is Karen and I am celery green. I'm healthy, crunchy, and I love peanut butter."

The color choices are unique and individual, and other group members typically remember them. This exercise helps get people to step out of their standard introductions and helps them connect on a level that is interesting, fun, and memorable, and it is a great way to kick off the first group meeting.

The quality of group members' success often equals the quality of questions that are asked, challenges that are given, and truths that are told. If you want to achieve more, be and do more, the quickest, easiest, and surest route to success is to ask better, bigger questions!

In order for wisdom to emerge, powerful questioning and active listening needs to take place in the coaching group. Learning to ask a concise and powerful question and then to be quiet and actively listen to the response is a great way to learn more about individuals in the group. That is the model that allows group members to fully explore a situation and communicate effectively with their peers.

Asking powerful questions in a group is the ability to ask to reveal the information needed for maximum benefit to the coaching client and the group (ICF core competencies).

1. Powerful questions focus on creating the future rather than present or future dilemmas.
2. Asking powerful questions leads to new and better ways of evoking clarity and awareness.
3. Powerful questions foster an environment of discovery where ideas and creative solutions are spawned.
4. Powerful questions in a group take inquiry to a deeper, more meaningful conversation.

Experience and Knowledge Collection Systems

Before the first meeting:
- Interview group participants individually by phone or e-mail to explore the opportunities, responsibilities, and commitments of joining a group.
- Send group members your welcome packet including thoughtful questions and ask them to respond via e-mail prior to the group.
- Share the answers of the thoughtful question with the group prior to the first meeting. (Make sure to ask each group member's permission first.)
- Look up group member's websites and share the link with the other members of the new group.
- Check out group members' biographies and website messages and focus.
- Connect group participants before their first meeting by collecting and sharing their pictures, bios, and thoughtful questions in a group coaching portfolio.

During the group coaching meeting:
- Listen for and highlight wisdom as it is being shared in the group.
- Acknowledge group members for engaging actively with each other and highlighting some of the gems that were shared.
- Create a "group wisdom" folder and save valuable e-mails from group members both positive and negative.
- Ask permission to coach a group member or share information an individual has communicated to you privately.
- Intentionally elicit "just in time" input and expertise from group members.
- Create a vacuum and hold the space open for wisdom to appear.
- Ask for a specific commitment for actions to be taken before the next meeting.
- End the call by asking each member what they have learned or will take away from the call that day.

After the group coaching session:
- Send a follow-up e-mail providing information, key insights from the meeting, and reminders of their next meeting date and time.
- Highlight the questions asked and the value shared during the session.

- Encourage others to share any shifts or breakthroughs they experienced after the group meeting by e-mail or telephone.
- Encourage group members to connect outside of the group sessions.
- Allow the coach to let go of the need to be the expert

Asking powerful questions takes pressure off the coach to provide external value, solve a problem, or teach. It takes responsibility off the coach to change group members or their circumstances and allows them to discover and create their own solutions. Coaches sometimes feel the need to impress with long explanations or lessons, and asking powerful questions automatically bypasses that temptation.

Case Study—Judy Feld

Judy Feld, MCC, has been successfully coaching groups for many years. She calls this group connection a "common thread" and shares an example below. With the common thread, Judy can be confident that the questions she asks in the group are not only relevant to a particular participant, but are of universal interest and importance.

One of the most important factors in attracting ideal clients into a coaching group and ensuring that the group is sustainable and long-running, is to have what I generally refer to as a "common thread." More specifically, this "common thread" can be:

- The same profession or occupation, e.g. attorneys or engineers.
- A common interest or situation, e.g. career transition or retirement.
- Based on trends and "hot coaching topics," with recognition of perceived needs in the marketplace, a unique finely-tuned niche and the ability to find people in it, or a very specific specialty area for your coaching.

This model focuses on a long-running group of female scientists, gathered from all over the United States and Canada and meeting virtually twice a month. To further differentiate the common thread, the participants are from the private sector, as contrasted with university faculty. (I have another similar leadership group for women in academia.)

I'll focus this example on one participant, Melissa, a PhD biologist working in a hospital system on the West Coast. Her experience illustrates the rich growth possibilities inherent in the group experience, including the wisdom, feedback, and questions from the other group members in addition to my coaching of the group.

Melissa joined the group to improve her assertiveness, leadership, and communication skills, and to gain increased confidence in dealing with sometimes intimidating physicians and hospital administrators. She began seeing positive progress very soon, both in the intended areas and also with issues that came to the surface when raised by other group members. Some specific examples, in Melissa's words:

- **Communication**: "I increasingly learned how to communicate clearly about what I wanted in a direct, calm, non-confrontational manner and in words that felt comfortable to me. In fact, Judy (and the group) sometimes helped me to find the words I most wanted to use, and they were more effective than my habitual patterns."
- **Negotiation/Confidence**: "My skills in negotiating and in saying what I want in a relaxed, clear manner have increasingly improved, as has my confidence—gifts that I have applied with great success in both my personal and work life."
- **Career Development**: "Coaching has been invaluable in helping me to navigate over the years from one interesting work situation to another, and to clearly identify what I wanted to do, instead of accepting what seemed to be available or what was the most logical next step in my career. In each case, I was able to craft the type of work I wanted and to receive excellent compensation for it. I have created more time for gardening, which I love, and noticed much less stress in my life."
- **Value of Coaching**: "I find Judy's help to be prompt, specific, gentle, and perceptive. She has enabled me to more clearly identify my strengths and the type of work I most wanted to do."

To meet the needs of Melissa and the other group members (of varied ages, backgrounds, and objectives) we adhere to the following structure:

- There is time for each group member to be coached in each session.
- The coach is able to react and respond to participants' questions and requests.
- There is a topic selected for each group session, with the time to vary by the needs of the group.
- Each session will be different; there is no rigid agenda, curriculum, or mold.

Judy Feld

Master Certified Coach, Certified Mentor Coach
Author of *SmartMatch Alliances*
Past President, International Coach Federation
Cofounder, Executive and Professional Coaching Program, University of Texas at Dallas
http://www.coachingsuccess.com

judy@coachnet.com

Coaching Questions

1. Are you creating groups where the individuals share a "common thread"?
2. Do you give every group member the opportunity to ask questions and make comments often?
3. How do you make sure the agenda stays relevant and engaging?
4. Are you asking questions that challenge and inspire group members?
5. Do you end each group meeting with thought-provoking questions?

Chapter Eight
Full Group Engagement

"To be fully engaged we must be physically energized, emotionally connected, mentally focused, and spiritually aligned with a purpose beyond our own self interest."
—From the book *The Power of Full Engagement*,
by Jim Loehr and Tony Schwartz

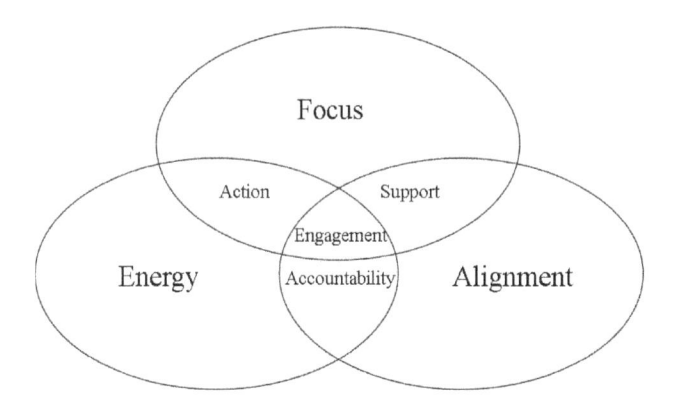

```
              Focus
         Action    Support
            Engagement
    Energy  Accountability  Alignment
```

The Three Levels of Full Group Engagement

People join coaching groups primarily to achieve a desired end result. Even though a group member may initially join with the intention of achieving only their individual goals, they quickly recognize that as they receive the help and encouragement they need, they are expected and encouraged to contribute to the success of others. As the group evolves from an unformed group of individuals seeking personal achievement and becomes a formed group of interactive and interdependent members, participants understand that they have a vested interest in supporting and encouraging other members to achieve the outcomes they want. The process of bonding and investment creates an environment where full group engagement can occur.

When the group is fully engaged on many levels by participating, contributing, and relating, it creates energy, enthusiasm, and accountability that permeates the group; and an environment is created where successful goal achievement can happen easily and naturally. The members often experience irresistible involvement. Those who are typically "side sitters" are drawn into participation in the group by the space created by the coach for every participant to contribute as well as craft an opportunity to spotlight specific contributions.

In order to have that full engagement, the group members must also have a clear focus about what they want to achieve as a group. Creating a group mission statement that inspires and motivates the group and creates a clear strategy for accomplishing that mission is key to the group's success. By clearly knowing what they want to achieve, the group can stay focused and check in regularly to evaluate if they are "on mission."

A good mission statement is inspiring, exciting, clear, and engaging. Co-creating that mission for the group requires each member to bring their wisdom to the group discussion and use the proficiency of laser speaking to keep that mission to no more than one sentence.

In her book, *The Path*, Laurie Beth Jones says a mission statement should have definite criteria. It should be:

1. No longer than one sentence.
2. Easily understood by a twelve-year-old.
3. Recited by memory at gunpoint. If group members co-create a mission statement that is universally inspiring, the odds of them being fully engaged increase exponentially.

One of the premises in *The Power of Full Engagement* is that life is not a marathon but actually a series of sprints. Recognizing and developing sprint goals allows full group engagement to be carried out in sprints. Periodization is a great model I use with some group members to help them set sprint goals. This helps them prepare and execute by focusing on one business strategy at a time before taking a break and then choosing a new focus. They feel as if they are training for the Olympics.

Group coaching is a great manifestation of the power of this concept. People frequently join coaching groups in order to accomplish something specific in a finite amount of time. Often people come to the group who have had the intention of accomplishing a goal for a long time but haven't succeeded on their own. Joining others on a clear mission for achievement raises the odds for success.

Example from a financial coaching group

Debbie Curtis: "I have been trying to reach the Million Dollar Round Table (MDRT) goal for fifteen years, and it wasn't until I joined the MDRT coaching group that I was able to achieve it—in the first year."

Debbie is a part of an ongoing MDRT group with a strong internal mission. That mission was for all the members to reach the Million Dollar Round Table, of which only about 3% of financial industry representatives reach. She sprinted to the finish of her production year using coaching and her peer group member's support and encouragement. Even after reaching that pinnacle, she wants to replicate her accomplishment and maintain those standards, so she remains committed to her group. Her group has been so successful that they have expanded their mission. That expanded mission includes each member of their peer group becoming a sponsor for other agents in company groups targeting the MDRT goal. Debbie continues to encourage and inspire others while raising her own personal bar to move to the next plateau in her business.

Distinctions in Full Group Engagement: Isolation vs. Sense of Community

Keys for group members to become fully engaged

While the coach is on a mission to collect a group of individuals and create a highly functioning and interactive group, individual members also take responsibility for their own mission.

One model that has worked well with my coaching groups is for the members to hold additional meetings without the coach. This gives added value to the group members who want to participate and facilitates more participation, accountability, and connection for group members.

Fully engaged members typically:

- Are willing to be playful, to grow, experiment, and share with others.
- Design the group meetings and agendas.
- Create a group plan to succeed.
- Come to the call prepared to participate and ask for what they want.
- Make commitments to the group and are accountable for those commitments.

- Learn to coach and support each other, rather than advise.
- Attend every call and arrive on time prepared.
- Commit to the success of the others as well as their own success.
- Honor each other by fully listening, being truthful, and maintaining confidentiality.

Another full engagement strategy is for the group members to challenge each other to ensure there is accountability and follow through. When individuals are on a quest to achieve a big athletic goal, they typically hire a coach and a team of professionals to support this quest.

Bonnie Blair is a fabulous example of this athletic model, as I described in chapter 3. She brought not only her coach and trainer team to the Olympics, but all her friends and family to help her to achieve the goal of winning more gold medals than any other woman before her in the Winter Olympics. By creating a support team and a group of supporters, you can increase your odds of succeeding exponentially.

Dr. Rensis Likert, a well-known management researcher, said, "The greater the loyalty of a group toward the group, the greater is the motivation among the members to achieve the goals of the group."

From my perspective, this is a moment in time when individuals are fiercely independent and intensely collaborative. That also resonates as the criteria in a coaching group. Group members want to achieve something personally and be responsible for their own success and achievements, while at the same time they want to contribute and collaborate with their peers to speed up the process and raise the odds for success.

Full Group Engagement Story

In 1999, a group of women in financial services joined a coaching group with the intention of establishing a strong financial services business and increase their yearly production so that they all become "Championship Producers." This group became a fully engaged group very quickly and effectively.

During the first month and a half, the women became a formed group. Two women in the group knew each other from home office meetings before the group formed, and their connection was a catalyst for helping the group move into trust and intimacy very quickly.

Another woman who joined the group was very motivated and driven. She had recently divorced and was a single mother with a small son. She wanted to produce enough income to afford to hold on to her home on her own and to achieve financial stability and success for herself and her child.

Liz's energy, drive, and relentless commitment to success had a profound effect on all the group members.

Each member had created her vision, mission, and specific goals for success in this yearlong coaching group, so they moved quickly into full group engagement. They made it a badge of honor to attend all meetings. We heard a helicopter in the background as one of the members attended a political rally where her husband was introducing the governor. She put the call on mute and stepped into a side room to listen and occasionally participate. She was determined not to miss her group meeting. Another member called in to her coaching group from a resort hotel in Mexico while on vacation to share her achievements and to ask for support on her next big hurdle.

At the midpoint of the year for the group, Liz suggested that they make their reservations collectively in the hotel where the championship invitees were staying that year. She said she was putting "a line in the sand" by saying no matter what happened, they were *all* going to make championship together. Everyone in the group agreed, and they all booked flights to the meeting and reserved adjoining hotel rooms. At the end of the year, all of the group members qualified, received invitations, and celebrated their success at the championship meeting. Several in the group acknowledged that working for the championship was merely a wish for them until they joined the coaching group and then made that commitment and were accountable to their group.

Case Study: Full Group Engagement
Helping Ordinary People do Extraordinary Things

The Company: A US-based Fortune 100 global manufacturing company with locations in North America, Europe, Asia, and Latin America.

The Project: Create a centralized purchasing function in twelve major business units by June 2008, critical for company growth and closely watched by the CEO as well as Wall Street analysts.

The Group: An implementation team was formed comprised of two groups. The members of Group A were project leaders implementing new purchasing processes in the field branches. The members of Group B were system analysts migrating multiple ancient purchasing systems to a state-of-the-art procurement system.

The group's challenges:
1. Quickly develop trust, commitment, and accountability as a single team or group.
2. Get the buy-in of the branch management and field purchasing staff to make major changes.

November 27, 2007—Day One, Morning
The group got together for a one-and-a-half-day kickoff. Some participants arrived early, some late. Most turned on their computers or regularly checked text messages. They sat with their buddies. The members listened politely to the chief procurement officer's speech about how important they were and how important the project was to the future of the company. During breaks they would privately talk about all the reasons why the project wouldn't work and the lack of resources preventing them from being successful by June 2008.

November 27, 2007—Day One, Afternoon
Group coaching would be a key part of the six-month project. Coach Marie began with new ground rules for group accountability: computers and phones must be turned off; everyone must show respect for meeting times; and everyone must follow a safe process so that all issues and concerns were brought to the group. Individual sidebars were not allowed! The rest of the day focused on each person's strengths and unique talents to integrate the two groups.

November 28, 2007—Day Two, Morning
The group's energy shifted from how the project couldn't be done to how it could be accomplished. Using laser coaching to get through the rough spots, roles, responsibilities, authority, and timelines were agreed upon in two hours—a first!

January 2008
It's the first group-coaching call and they are in crisis. Several didn't follow through on their December commitments. Group B's manager can't let go of approving everything. Two new leaders are emerging, causing jealousy among their peers. After reminding the team to use the group to be accountable and achieve something extraordinary, the group worked through the issues. Whew!

February 2008
The members are using group coaching with their branch project teams. With their strong unified approach and a major win from the toughest

critic, the group is ahead of schedule. One member just couldn't follow through with his commitments and was voted out.

March 2008
The group coaching now focuses on tough issues. Members trust asking for what they need or want.

June 2008
Success! Twelve business units with fifty-six branches are fully implemented.

December 2008
The company was expecting ten million dollars in savings in 2008, and they realized a savings of more than forty million dollars! Three members were promoted.

Coach Marie Guthrie
CEO of Legacy Track
Marie Guthrie Personal Success Coach LLC
coach@marieguthrie.com
www.marieguthrie.com

Coaching Questions

1. Do you keep your antenna up for gauging the energy level of the group?
2. Have you identified one or two members of the group who will participate immediately if you can feel the group disengaging?
3. Are you keeping a list of powerful questions that you can use to inspire participation?
4. Are you prepared for the group changing the agenda in the middle of the group?
5. Are you checking in with the group regularly to encourage spontaneity?

Chapter Nine
Collaborative Agendas—Group-Based Content

"A group of individuals may stimulate one another in the creation of ideas."
—Estill I. Green, American Business Executive,
VP of Bell Telephone Laboratories

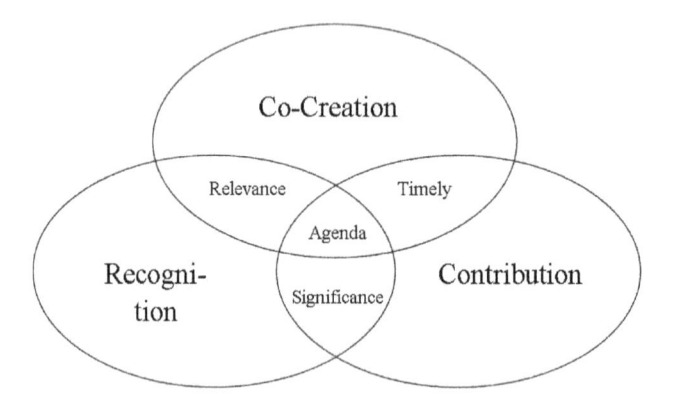

[Venn diagram: three overlapping circles labeled "Co-Creation", "Recognition", and "Contribution"; intersections labeled "Relevance", "Timely", "Significance", with "Agenda" at the center.]

The agendas in group coaching are not driven primarily by coach-based content, but rather from the typical coach and client relationship of "just in time" needs and wants of the group participants. The group is typically formed with either a company or organizational focus created from a strategic initiative or from group members' focus on a goal they all want to achieve. The company focus may vary from sales to the contributions, depending on the shifting needs and collaboration of the group coaching members. A coach proficient at co-creating the group agenda gets out of the way so the members can play a powerful part and take ownership in the group coaching experience. The agenda is then based on the needs and desires of the group members as they focus on achieving their goals.

A good example is an affiliated group that has joined together to serve as a board of directors (BOD) for each other. A part of the commitment to their group is that they regularly bring specific real-life agenda items to the call. Recently, one of the members brought an agenda item that needed group input. His office manager of twenty-five years was retiring, and she wanted to return one or two days a week to work part time for him. He had very mixed feelings about how that might work and wanted the input of his BOD peers before he made his decision. He sent his agenda item to me as the coach, and I added it to the agenda for our next meeting. A few days before we met, I sent out the agenda to the members so they could peruse it ahead of time and add any items they wanted.

When the group met, Trent explained the circumstances just a little more, and then the group shared their personal experience and wisdom with him. I coached him individually in the group to help him clarify his concerns and priorities. Then we had a round-robin, where everyone in the group asked questions and shared insights. By the end of the call, he had gained clarity on the situation with the great input from everyone, and he felt confident that after careful consideration, he would make the right decision. It was a valuable experience not only for Trent, but for all the group members.

Co-creating the agenda requires group members to be on the calls, fully participating and willing to share business and life circumstances that are real and important to them. Also, if the group has chosen a quarterly focus like increased production, implementing more efficient office systems, getting higher quality referrals, or delegating 30 percent more of their responsibilities, there may be some content and resources supplied by the coach and members of the group.

There may also be some reading and researching or tracking and reporting that members do to achieve their specific outcomes. All of those exercises will be custom designed for that individual group member and their own leadership team. Group members may also ask for and receive some individual laser coaching with their coach to overcome personal obstacles or design follow-through strategies to accomplish what they wish to achieve. They also may want to share confidential situations with the coach that they would be uncomfortable sharing with the entire group.

Co-creating the agenda requires the coach to lead the group in creating a collaborative environment where everyone takes ownership of the group so that they can step up and ask for what they want and contribute honestly and openly. This group ownership is essential for group members in developing interdependent relationships that foster their personal and professional development while allowing them to support and encourage others in that quest. It is possible to have specific prepared content that you offer to groups when a subject comes up, but let the need for the content arise from the group, not simply because you as the coach have something you have created and have a need or desire to share.

The coach must maintain a coaching presence for this shared ownership to occur. Instead of the coach owning the group and leading the group focus and interaction, the coach partners with the group to create a collaborative and creative environment that fosters full interaction. As a result, the coach remains fully present and flexible during the group meeting, using intuition and experience to change and adapt as the group co-creates.

It also requires the coach to have the courage to challenge someone who attempts to change the focus by asking the questions that evoke responses from the group to clarify if the change in direction is agreed to by everyone. Using powerful questions and listening to all the participants' responses allows the coach to make sure no one is left out of the conversation and that the group moves forward in agreement. The coach can also make individual coaching time available for members who want and need some personal coaching that is not of universal concern and relevance to all the group members.

> Being part of Group J has been extremely significant in not only my personal but professional life. The encouragement and experience of each member of the group has been invaluable in helping me reach my business goals. The integrity of the group and the support from each member has been not only inspiring, but has helped me bring clarity to my vision of my business. We all come from different backgrounds and experiences. This has only helped to make our group stronger. We support each other and also help hold each other accountable. My business would not be where it is today if it were not for your guidance and coaching. I value everyone so much and am so proud to be affiliated with this group. We are now beginning our fourth year together, and I expect that this year will bring tremendous growth for all of us. I only hope that I have contributed to the group to the extent the group has contributed to me.
> **Candace, a financial services professional**

There are three stages of coaching groups when co-creating the agenda that is essential to the process. In the marketing and collection stage of group formation, it is important to have interaction with prospective group members to make sure they are on board with the focus of the group and that they are willing to collaborate with the other group members.

Here are some ways you can find out if a prospective member is right for the group:

1. Set up interviews with prospective group coaching members and ask strategic questions.

   Examples of overview questions:
   - What is the focus in your business this year?
   - What is your most pressing need?
   - What do you want most in your business? In your life?
   - What is your biggest business challenge?
   - What is your biggest dream?
   - How would you contribute to helping the other business owners in your group?
   - (Limit questions to five or six.)

2. Set up an online survey for prospective members.
3. Design a research and development group that encourages participation and contribution.
4. Establish teleforums—free information forums to give prospects a group experience.
5. Create brainstorming sessions that allow prospects to share their ideas and resources.

Observe how prospects interact in group settings, such as classes or teleclasses. Once the group is formed, it is important that members take the challenge to create meaningful group meetings in the second stage by:

1. Responding to the coach's request for agenda items with relevant topics.
2. Keeping the group connected and communicating with their fellow group members.
3. Completing their coach preparation form and returning prior to the group calls.
4. Sharing specific successes and concerns that affect progress toward goals.
5. Encouraging and acknowledging group peers when individual contributions are made.

Session agenda example
- Laser check in (all group members participate).
- Most successful achievement of the last two weeks.

- Most challenging experience of the last two weeks.
- Questions for group discussion (group members participate as needed or desired).
- Current opportunities and possibilities.
- Impeding decisions that member needs coaching on or input from group.
- Industry trends or changes that affect group members.
- Challenges that need to be addressed.
- Coaching tips that are applicable.
- Laser roundup.
- How was this call valuable for you?
- What are you taking away from the session today?

The third stage of co-creation is retention in the group.
1. The coach and the group keep the agenda relevant and current.
2. Group members regularly co-create wisdom, coach, and support each other, and share resources, experiences, and connections.
3. Peers take ownership in the group, recommit to the group, and "re-imagine" what is possible for the group regularly.
4. Group members are responsible for co-creating valuable group meetings, and the coach is responsible for providing highly skilled, high-end coaching (versus training, advising, facilitating, or managing).

There is a clear distinction between allowing input and contributions in the group, and the group members owning their group and, thus, being primarily responsible for the focus, content, and wisdom in the group. This process depends on a peer relationship within the group. Everyone has a significant role. The coaching role is:

Co-creating versus acceptance
- Is mutual and proactive.
- Instills a sense of ownership in the group members.
- Requires that the group coach trust the environment and encourage co-creation by honoring and valuing input.
- Forces the group coach to give up her or his own agenda.
- Establishes a framework for a collaborative process that builds on itself.
- Establishes the ability to go back again and co-create again when something isn't working.

- Is a shared team-oriented ongoing exercise.
- Allows input, soliciting ideas from participants.
- Is permission-based; the coach determines when and how the participants can share ideas.
- Instills a sense of hierarchy in the group with the coach on top, in charge.
- Requires that the coach is responsible for everything on the group agenda.
- Establishes a framework for a process that needs to be recreated in every session.

1. Ownership versus participation
Ownership Group
- Group members feel responsible for creating valuable group experiences for themselves and each other.
- The group develops interdependence.
- The coach is free to just be the group coach and can point out shifts in the members and in the group.
- By being a neutral observer, the coach brings the greatest value through active listening, hearing all that is said and unsaid, and recognizing and highlighting the uniqueness of each member.

Participation Group
- Group members feel responsible solely for their own individual experience.
- The group bonds around the coach versus with each other.
- The coach is solely responsible for keeping the group's agenda and monitors accountability.

2. Co-created agenda versus content
Co-created Agenda
- In a co-created agenda, the group meetings are flexible and based on the immediate needs of the group members.
- Group meetings are not a set predictable program but are dynamic and fluid.
- A co-created agenda forces the coach to let go of full ownership of the group. That allows the group coaching to establish a coaching presence so they are the coach, not the leader.

- Group members provide requests based on their real experiences and co-create content with the coach based on their specific needs for "just in time" learning.

Content Based
- A content-based group has a set topic scheduled and outlined by the coach for each group session.
- The coach retains ownership of the group and teaches and leads the group.

Case Study—Group Coaching—The All4One Approach from Jay Perry, MCC

About five years ago I received a call from a prospective client who wanted to be in a coaching group with me as the coach. I told the prospect that I was ready to stop coaching groups altogether; that I had been leading groups for twenty-five years, and they never quite met my expectations. They were never long enough, deep enough, or committed enough to meet my needs. The prospect, being a coach, asked me what kind of group I wanted to lead. I described a group that would connect deeply at a retreat and authentically commit to work with each other and me for an entire year. The prospect said, "Great, sign me up!" And so All4One coaching groups were born (www.jayperry.com).

The key to this approach is to establish a flow of generosity, where group members are not only able and willing to give, but able and willing to identify and ask for what they need.

I love this approach for the community it builds and for the magic that it is able to create. As the lead coach, I may start out as the focal point for organization and inspiration, but as time goes by the group naturally forms other bonds of coaching, advising, supporting, training, sharing, supporting, inspiring, and participating.

Here are a few stories from a group that's been together well past the initial first-year commitment that illustrates that matrix's magic:

> Some would call me a "solopreneur." Yet All4One has taken the "solo" out of my entrepreneurial adventure. In addition to the wisdom and experience of our mentor coach, Jay, on a regular basis I get to contribute to and avail myself of a wealth of information and resources; diverse skill sets, multiple perspectives and approaches to any given situation, and the amazing generosity and commitment of several

colleagues, both in the group setting and separately one-on-one. It isn't always easy to be surrounded by a group of your peers who specialize in personal and professional excellence and development and who are holding you to the task, while you are doing the same for them, but the willingness to be honest, vulnerable, and educable when held within the fierce and loving embrace of our group only speaks to the trust and compassion that we have developed for ourselves and for each other. And this dedicated practice, I am certain, makes us all better professionals—and better human beings.
Susan

Jay Perry, MCC
Mentor Coach and Founder
The Coaching Collective
perryochs@shasta.com

> **Coaching Questions:**
> 1. Can you be comfortable trusting group coaching members to collaborate in creating the groups' agenda?
> 2. Are you willing as the coach to give up your own agenda for the group?
> 3. Do you see your primary role as being the coach for the group?
> 4. Are you open to coaching a group for several years rather than limiting groups to several months?
> 5. Can you give up directing and being in control of your coaching groups?

Chapter Ten

Championing the Group

"It's the coach's job to hold up your goal, shine the light on your path, and say, 'Yes, but what about this?'"
—Health *magazine*

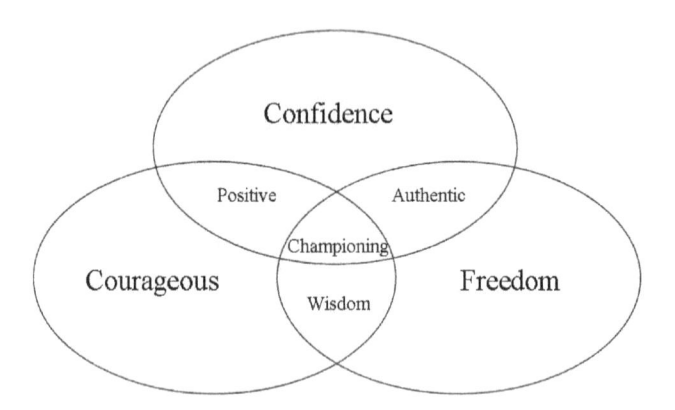

Venn diagram showing three overlapping circles labeled Confidence, Courageous, and Freedom. Overlaps are labeled Positive, Authentic, Championing, and Wisdom.

The coaching process is designed for the purpose of establishing a peer relationship with our clients so that they have a partner, a mentor, a guide, and an advocate. The standard for top athletes is to always have a coach. As coaches, we literally lead from our clients. So we champion who they are and what they want, and then we help them develop a strategy for personal and professional growth and co-create a strategy in their pursuit of their dreams and goals. Group coaches have the added opportunity and challenge to coach and champion not only our individual clients, but also all the members within a group.

The word "championing" is often used in context with leaders choosing a strategy for their focus or intention within an organization. Example: "The new CEO is championing change in the organization." For group and team members, having their advocates and coach champion for their success in an organization can make a difference in their career path as well as the quality of their lives.

In credentialing coaching groups, I was able to give one of the coaches going for the International Coach Federation Master Certified Coach certification a direct critique while still championing him!

I listened to a recording of the coach coaching a client, and instead of saying, "You sounded more like a consultant than a coach," I said, "I know that you have a PhD in psychology, but when I listened to the recording of you coaching a client, I wouldn't have imagined in a million years that you had *ever* been a therapist. It is really amazing how you can step out of the therapist role so completely and effortlessly." Then I asked him, "Can you articulate for me the difference between a coach and a psychologist?" He did an amazing job and I said, "That is a brilliant distinction between the two. You really have absolute clarity on the similarities and differences."

Then I said, "I have another request for you. Can you please tell me the distinctions between a coach and a consultant?" He stammered a few minutes without being able to explain clearly the distinction. The feedback I gave him was, "As soon as you have the same clarity between a coach and consultant that you have between a coach and therapist, you can be certain you will always show up as a coach when that is your role without anyone knowing that you have ever been a consultant." That conversation created an awareness that allowed him to make the shift needed so that he was able to show up with his clients and on the MCC exam as a masterful coach.

One of the main ways coaches can champion their clients is by mastering the art of masterful feedback. A coach in a 12 Keys coaching group, Clair Ferguson from the UK, recently shared, "A Guide to Giving Positive Feedback in a Group."

1. It is important to give positive feedback in the moment

The instant you become aware that someone has done something you feel merits positive feedback, tell him or her about it. If you wait until later it typically has much less impact.

"Did everyone hear the comment David just made? Doesn't that really sum up the conversation with a powerful synopsis?" As the coach of the group, you can make a note while you are listening to group members so that you can give the feedback to a group member while it is appropriate and relevant.

2. Give positive feedback in terms of your feelings and your opinion, not as a judgment or critique

I might say, "It was meaningful to me the way you took responsibility for your mistake and apologized immediately," rather than, "You handled that situation well." The former gives them your input about the effect the group member's apology had, rather than just a general comment or observation. The latter comment suggests that you are some sort of authority in how the situation was handled and insinuates you have the right to grade their performance. The two of you are peers and sharing opinions is a collegiate exercise.

3. Be specific about what it is you are encouraging.

If you are actively listening to the group member describe an interaction with a client that went especially well, you could make a very specific and authentic comment. You might say, "Helping your client navigate through a difficult course by encouraging her to identify several possible options, you demonstrated your professional expertise and commitment by looking out for her best interest while allowing her to emerge confident about making her own decisions."

Another example might be, "I really admire the way you handled that situation just now with Laura. It was so thoughtful and supportive." This is an example of a specific praise that will help the client recognize the behavior they exhibited and that you observed as effective.

4. Do not over-praise the group or individuals.

People will be wary if the praise you give is not proportional to what they did or said. "You're a fantastic financial professional" is so vague and full of hyperbole. "Wow, several of your comments today were incredibly memorable!" may not sound realistic and genuine.

While "I agree with Sara, the illustration you gave was helpful not only to her, but to me as well, thank you very much for sharing your wisdom," will, often, please someone who has just gone out of their way to contribute in the group.

5. Practice championing your clients and your groups regularly and consistently

Coaches who champion group members put up their antenna and listen for all the opportunities to highlight, spotlight, and encourage group members to contribute. The more a coach advocates for the group, the more group members learn to champion the group and to be an advocate for themselves.

By listening actively and making notes when a group member rises to a challenge, follows through on a commitment, contributes something of value, and shares it with their group, or when a group member is especially kind and thoughtful, a group coach will find championing becomes a natural and integral part of her or his groups.

Group Exercise

It can be helpful to ask someone to step up to receive feedback from the group and have someone play the cheerleading role of feedback. You might hear, "You are a fantastic manager," or "You are doing a great job for us," rather than giving the person specific, positive championing feedback. This is a great opportunity to ask a group member to step up and give specific positive feedback to the group member. Example: "You manage your team so well that one of your team members shared that you make her feel essential to overall team success."

One other observation is how astonishing it is to see how seldom high achievers celebrate and acknowledge their own successes. One of the great opportunities a coach has in a group is to help design an environment where each group member can share and celebrate their individual achievements shamelessly!

Championing
1. A specific reference to a group member's success, strength, or gift, not a general comment.
2. Encouraging the rest of the group to celebrate the member's success.
3. Highlight a success as a reminder for each member to celebrate his or her own successes.
4. People are more likely to receive and acknowledge championing if it is based in truth.

Cheerleading
1. An emotional reaction and comment that may not be based in reality.
2. Cheerleading may come from a coach's needs and attachment to the groups' success in an appropriate and meaningful way.

3. Cheerleading is often a generalization that may not appear to be sincere or appropriate.
4. Cheerleading typically doesn't encourage and inspire members of a group.

Why is this important?

If we don't have permission to celebrate achievements by acknowledging our own success, it is difficult for a coach to champion others. If we move on to "what's next" before we celebrate a success, we end up feeling a lack of satisfaction and joy in our achievements. It is important to celebrate our own successes, and here are some examples for self-championing you can share with your groups.

1. Keep a daily journal, review it periodically, and make a note of specific progress that's been achieved.
2. Schedule personal celebration time as part of your regularly self-care routine.
3. Acknowledge your accomplishments on a regular basis. **Exercise from *Strategic Coach*, Dan Sullivan's Focus 21 Program:** Every evening, for twenty-one days, instead of creating a to-do list, write down five things you've accomplished today and how you can expand those accomplishments.
4. Create a self-championing ritual.
   a. Schedule the time and place for a celebration.
   b. Invite others to be a part of this ceremony.
   c. Dancing (literally or metaphorically).

Jeanne was a member of an affiliated group of financial services representatives. She had joined a financial services company with a background in education with the intention of challenging herself. She had no idea how hard establishing her own business would be. In fact, she was struggling significantly when she joined a group of five women representatives with a coach and a successful mentor. Despite her best intentions and hard work, she continued to struggle with marketing and running her own business. In fact, she was questioning whether this business was right for her at all.

In a group meeting, I asked Jeanne if there was something she had always wanted to do but had never had the courage. She said she had always wanted to parachute out of an airplane. I asked her how that might impact her business. She thought about it and shared that she believed it would help her be more courageous. At our next group meeting, she told us that she had decided to schedule a plane at a local airport and attend the jumping program. One of her group members, Teresa, announced that if Jeanne was going to parachute out of a plane, she wanted to be there for her and waiting for her to land.

The entire group encouraged and supported her as she stepped out of her comfort zone to parachute out of a plane. Teresa was a true champion for Jeanne when she flew to Phoenix and went with her to the airport. Teresa was standing there in the landing area, cheering and taking pictures as Jeanne jumped out of that airplane, spread her arms in exhilaration, and landed safely.

That act of courage was a defining moment in Jeanne's life and career. With newfound courage, she set out with determination to establish a successful business. She shared that without her coaching group, that dream for being an entrepreneurial financial professional would never have happened. She was honored with a bronze award for production and service at the annual national conference at the end of that year and continues to be a successful businesswoman.

Case study for championing in a group from a financial services group that was together for four years.

There is a synergy that seems to come out of groups where the facilitator becomes a coach to pull the group wisdom into the center and then to spread that out among all members. There's also sort of "running in the pack" mentality where people sometimes won't try their limits if you are coaching them individually, but if you're coaching them among their peers and some of the people they see as peers are working hard and trying harder just doing different things, that often takes that person beyond themselves.

"People say things, and it will trigger something in me, and I'll have a realization about another way it could be interpreted or a way what they just said can be applied to the broader circumstances of the group," Jeffrey shared.

As the coach, because you are outside the group and yet deeply embedded in it, you are able to pick up nuances that people in the group can't do—one, because they are too close to it, but secondly because they don't have the distance that your coaching training gives you, and they probably don't have the same reference point of information as well. I get a lot out of the things that clients say that inspire insights in me that I then share back in the group.

What is most personally satisfying to you about group coaching?
The deepest satisfaction I get out of groups is watching people take up an idea that one of their peers has put in the middle. So, my view of a group, and I'll say this to the group when I first assemble them, is that everyone in that group, the group as a whole, probably has all the answers to every problem any one of them will ever face in their business situation. Generally they have life roles and life situations, and so when someone asks a question you feed it to the group, and you'll get answers.

There is enormous satisfaction in watching people evolve over time. Someone will be challenged on a staff level that they don't relate to their staff well, and someone else has got their act together in the group, and over time you'll watch the one who used to struggle get much better and better at it. And that's just enormously satisfying.

A group is a better environment in which to build self-esteem in a client, because you are able to endorse them in the group, recognize the value and the truth of what that person said in the group. They don't have to say anything; it's just in the presence. Now bear in mind I'm coaching by phone so they can't see each other—but there's an atmosphere there. Anyone who puts that truth in the middle and has that truth adopted by the group has got proof that twelve to fifteen other people like them think this is valuable. If they doubt themselves, there are thirteen people arguing that they shouldn't. Not that they do it verbally—there's just a sense that the group endorses the value of what they put in the middle.

Someone said that creating the coaching environment is a BS-free safe zone. That's very much what happens in group coaching, even more so than one-on-one coaching. One on one coaching is quite intimate, and people are prepared to be emotionally naked one-on-one. But group coaching requires people to join a nudist colony almost in terms of ego. When the group evolves to the point where everyone in the group accepts everyone else for who and what they are, the personalities start to flare, the information starts to flow, and the group goes to another level.

Peter Rowe
ProfiTune Business Systems
peter.rowe@profitune.com
www.profitune.com

Coaching Questions:
1. Are you confident enough in your coaching role that you can be the champion for the group and the members in it?
2. Do you acknowledge the value each member brings to the group?
3. Do you champion members regularly and authentically?
4. How do you encourage group members to be champions for each other?
5. Do you provide the encouragement and support for the group members to become their own champions?

Chapter Eleven

Laser Coaching

"Laser coaching is defined as a specialized coaching technique and approach that promotes quick alignment, a rapid sense of relief, and a way of quickly unblocking someone who may have felt stuck in their way of thinking for a long time."
—Thomas Leonard, a founder of the coaching industry

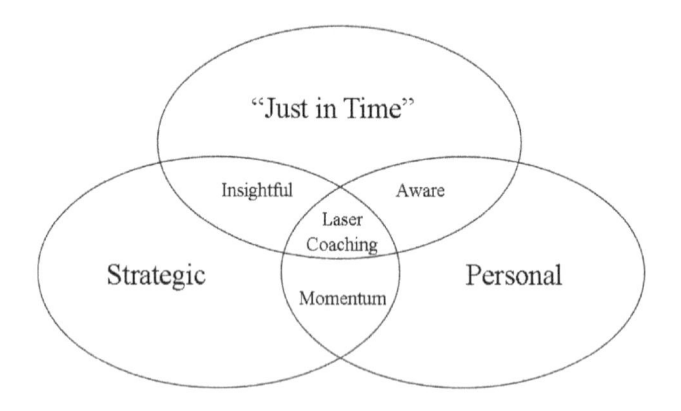

Laser coaching is one-to-one coaching specifically directed to working with a client to address a single issue, concern, opportunity, or challenge with individual clients. It can be used within the group as a whole so that group member can focus in on a specific issue. It can also be the perfect complement for group meetings by scheduling time that allows group members one-on-one time with the coach for concerns, opportunities, or personal development issues the group member may not want to share with everyone in the group.

Laser coaching is a great tool for groups because it is an instantaneous way to guide clients to their own answers within a group setting and allows coaching to occur strategically and quickly during a group meeting. The group coach can use the following five steps to help identify how to use laser coaching.

1. Identify and decide where laser coaching within a group client might be useful.
2. Create opportunities for individual coaching. Laser coaching can help a group member use both individual and group coaching opportunities. Example of a laser coaching question: In the present economic climate, are there three opportunities to expand your role in the company vs. remaining status quo?
3. Allow individuals to deal with a very personal or professional issue with the coach one-on-one that they may want to bring it to the group later but might choose the opportunity to run it by the coach first in a laser session.
4. Change perspective: Laser coaching gives an opportunity to coach around awareness and perspective in a short and strategy session.
5. By seeing that their situation is not unique, it allows group members to be reassured that they do not stand alone in their life circumstances. That can be enough to help them overcome a stalemate in their lives.

One of the best results of laser coaching is how the positive energy of the group can come from the momentum of the group. Laser coaching can provide the impetus for forward motion in a group member who is lagging behind in the group. That person getting back in stride and moving forward can create a real advantage for all group members.

Laser coaching within your coaching group

In group coaching, I set aside a laser coaching time at least once a month for all of my groups. I set up a two- to three-hour period of time on my calendar, and my virtual assistant sends the notification to the groups.

Clients in the group are asked to send an e-mail to me before a laser coaching meeting so that I know specifically what they want to focus on. They can either call in on an afternoon set aside for laser coaching (if I am coaching someone else, they leave a message, and I call them back during the two hours allotted), or they can reserve a time in fifteen-minute increments.

When I answer the phone, we both are ready to coach around that specific topic. It is amazing how when the intention is set and the client has clarified what they want to accomplish, the coaching can be very effective in a very short time period.

I offer laser coaching to all my groups—both external and company groups. Companies respond very favorably to the opportunity for individuals from the organization to have some individual, one-on-one coaching with me as their coach. More importantly, group members have the opportunity to connect with their coach in different and multiple coaching environments. Laser coaching is a real benefit for me as their coach because I get to know the group coaching clients better and, therefore, can become a better champion and coach for each member in the group and foster the connections between all the group members.

Laser coaching raises the skill for the coach by getting to the source of the problem. Despite the name, laser coaching may or may not shorten the coaching time, but it does make each coaching session more effective and efficient. Learning to recognize the "essence" and getting the client to move forward easily and skillfully is of invaluable benefit to clients.

The Process of Laser Coaching
1. The client identifies a specific concern, problem, opportunity, or stumbling block they want to be coached around.
2. The group client e-mails the coach the issue that they want to address in a laser coaching session before calling the coach.
3. The coach either sets an exact appointment time or calls in during the window of time the coach has reserved for group members.
4. The coach has the opportunity to read the e-mail and prepare for the group members' calls.
5. The client and coach have one focus for their laser meeting, so they maximize their time together and keep the client continuing to move forward.

Advantages for Laser Coaching
1. Group members who aren't moving forward due to an obstacle or lack of opportunity can have the opportunity to collaborate in a laser coaching session with their coach.
2. Group members find laser coaching encourages them to look at the change that may be valuable for them to make personally, rather than focusing on what is wrong with their boss, spouse, children, etc.

3. Laser coaching can help subtract a client's self-doubt and give them the courage to move forward.
4. Group members have the chance to use a coach to explore and discover opportunities rather than to receive advice.
5. The client often steps up to take responsibility for their choices.
6. If the client can't see any options, they can't move forward. If you have any doubt, ask yourself—and the client—"Is this really a problem?"
7. Clients' problems are probably not their exclusive problem. There are very few "unique" situations, so laser coaching with one member is typically relevant and helpful to the entire group.

Example of laser coaching with a financial services group coaching client who was new in the industry: (Identifying and coaching to the client's concern and obstacle.)

Coach: Congratulations on completing your fourteen days of arriving at the office by 8 AM! How does it make you feel to have completed that challenge?

Client: It is a great feeling—and I gave myself the reward. I got to go home three hours early on Thursday afternoon to play tennis in my league with no guilt. That was awesome!

Coach: To achieve your goal and reap the reward must feel terrific. Cool. Do you think arriving early is an established habit now?

Client: I am convinced it is, and I have a bet with my brother that will keep me focused on getting here early every day.

Coach: Excellent! What are we laser coaching about today?

Client: I wasn't able to phone more than one prospect today.

Coach: And did you have a phoning goal?

Client: Yes, my goal was to make ten calls today.

Coach: How important is that goal to you?

Client: Very. There are fifteen of us competing for two job opportunities, and the only way to make the cut is to phone and make appointments with prospects. So it is very important to me.

Coach: What prevented you from completing your calls?

Client: I stopped phoning after not reaching the first or second person I called.

Coach: What was the emotion that you experienced at that moment when you gave up phoning?

Client: I was frustrated and felt like dialing was useless if no one was in the office today.

Coach: Was that reaction based on an assumption or was it the truth?

Client: It was just what I felt, so I guess it was an assumption.

Coach: What are the odds that no one in the city was in the office today?

Client: That doesn't make sense, does it?

Coach: Not really. What has to happen to make sure you follow through on your calls tomorrow?

Client: I will sit down in the conference room at 9 AM tomorrow and not get up until I finish my ten calls.

Coach: Will you send me a text at the exact moment that you complete those calls?

Client: Really? Sure, I will send you a text each morning when I complete my calls this week. Is that okay?

Coach: Great! That sounds like a plan! I am looking forward to getting that text every day this week. I am confident this is going to be another successful week for you.

Thomas Leonard made the following statement in a teleclass: "The first step in laser coaching is to identify where lasering might be useful and ensure that the timing is right. The second step is to share a truth relating to their situation, and third is allowing the client to look at their situation in a new way. One of the benefits of this technique and approach is that you can help them get aligned more swiftly with their goal, feel a sense of relief faster, get unblocked faster, and move forward quickly. Most clients are stuck on something a lot of the time that's slowing them down, and you can laser coach to quickly help your clients become more 'superconductive.' I also use it with a client when they're in a situation where they're over their head and need to get back on track."

One of the ICF core competencies is direct communication. In the laser coaching opportunity, it is important to listen to and look for their strengths, values, purpose, and greatness as well as what is missing or what the client is avoiding, and communicate that directly.

Remember, this is not a forty-five-minute weekly coaching meeting, so the purpose is:

- To connect with your client immediately.
- Acknowledge a bright spot. (Something that has worked well for the client.)
- Listen for an opportunity.
- Ask one or more powerful questions.
- Challenge an assumption if they are making one.
- Create an awareness.
- Get a commitment for moving forward.

The more you practice the skill of laser coaching, the better you get. Laser coaching doesn't have to be breakthrough or life changing, just precise, accurate, sensitive, and helpful.

Case study on laser coaching—a breakthrough for a member with laser coaching?

There was a situation in a company where I coach groups, where a corporate group member, Nancy, came to a meeting and shared a frustration in her office. She explained that she had met with her manager, and he had given her an assignment that she was excited about.

Later, after another employee influenced him, he reconsidered. When Nancy's manager asked her what she thought about him reassigning the project to someone else, she said she didn't mind. As a result, he assigned it to the other person. Nancy expressed to her group how she felt a "little betrayed" and that she felt that this was an indication that maybe her manager couldn't be trusted and that he was more interested in playing politics than being supportive of his employees.

At first the group was supportive, with comments like, "I can understand why you are feeling this way" and "I know how you might be upset." I asked if we might do some laser coaching. After Nancy agreed, I asked the group if they could identify some assumptions that might be in play. Immediately, a group member commented that the manager might have made the assumption that it was all right to make the switch when he had asked her about changing his decision, and she had said it was okay. Another group member asked her how the manager could have known that she didn't really mean it when she said it was okay. Gradually, Nancy started questioning her judgment of her manager.

What emerged in less than five minutes of a laser coaching exchange was that Nancy recognized and acknowledged that she was clearly responsible for what happened with her manager. As a result, the following week she had a meaningful conversation with her manager, acknowledging her role in the situation. She reported to her group by e-mail that as a result of their talk, she and her supervisor had created a much stronger relationship based on an agreement to be honest in their communication. This exchange was not only valuable for Nancy, but caused members of the group to share how they had reassessed the times they had made assumptions causing them to misjudge situations. As a result of Nancy sharing her experience and laser coaching in her group, all her peers in the group benefited.

Cindy Petitt
Coaching for Positive Action
Petitt Consulting Practice, LLC
www.coachingforpositiveaction.com

Chapter Twelve
Creating Awareness

"I think self-awareness is probably the most important thing toward being a champion."
—Billie Jean King

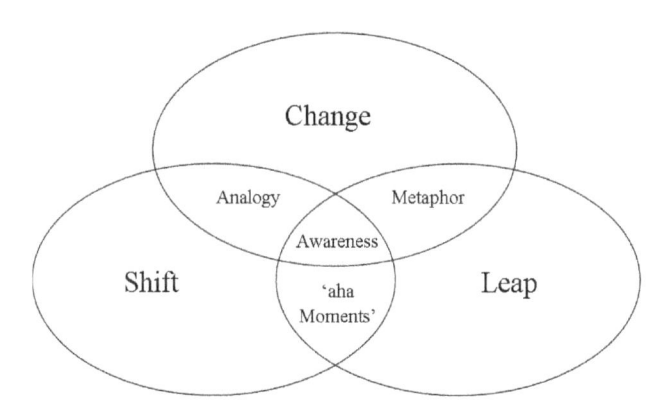

[Venn diagram with three overlapping ellipses labeled Change, Shift, and Leap. Overlapping regions labeled Analogy, Metaphor, Awareness, and 'aha Moments'.]

Group coaching presents a unique opportunity to become more self-aware by joining a group of peers who want to grow personally or professionally in a confidential and collaborative coaching environment. It is in that environment that people can become self-aware as well as becoming more aware of the world around them.

Questions for Group Members:
- How aware are you of all of the things going on around you?
- Do you understand how life works and how you are being affected?
- What is it that you wish you knew more about yourself?

Awareness

Awareness is one of the most valuable life skills a person can have. It's the ability to be present so that a person is hearing, seeing, observing, recognizing, and discerning the world around them and, therefore, being able to respond to what is happening from knowledge and reality. A person who is unaware often walks through life oblivious and unengaged. There are several levels of awareness, each of which clients can develop and enhance while working with an experienced coach. Awareness, for many, is the beginning of the journey to an emotionally and spiritually rich life.

By exploring our client's view of reality, a coach and a group can help a person take the steps to enhance and alter their situation. Acquiring awareness skills can make the difference between a client accepting life as it is and creating transcendental shifts that lead to a life where much more is possible.

Thomas Leonard, a founder of coaching, often referred to three stages for defining behavioral modification: a change, a shift, and a transformational leap. A change is a conscious decision to make an external behavioral change—in goals, in habits, etc. It can be temporary or permanent.

Hi Ginger,

Just this weekend I was thinking about some things we worked on in the group together as I was rafting down section four of the Chattooga River with two of my sons and my good friend, Bob. A few years ago, when you and I worked together on not only business opportunities and problems and priorities, but also integrating our business with my personal goals, I was able to change from my business being all consuming to a new perspective that I could grow my business while having a personal and family life. Members of the group helped me have the courage to make changes. That coaching brought some clarity, and when I was invited by Bob (who I didn't know too well at that time) to join him and two other guys on a backpacking trip in Colorado, I chose to go for it. I know I would have passed on the invitation before I worked with you. I would have believed that I was too busy to get away for ten days, but after coaching, I realized that I could delegate to my staff and take this opportunity for an adventure for myself.

> After that initial trip, we have become good friends with Bob and his wife, and I have had the pleasure of making friends with the two other guys we went with on that first backpacking trip. Since that first trip I have taken many more trips to Colorado with my new friends. As my sons have grown, I have taken them and climbed 14ers (mountains that are fourteen thousand feet high) with them. Last year we all went with our wives and the boys to the northwest. Bob, Jim (one of the friends I first met in Colorado), my oldest son, Sam, and I all climbed Mount Rainier. Dan, at fifteen, is one of the younger teens to have reached the summit of Mount Rainier.
>
> This past weekend, Bob, Sam, and my middle son, Ben, rafted on the Chattooga and then did "duckies" on the Nantahala. (Knowing your background, I am sure you're familiar with these rivers!) Last year we did the Okauchee River. Last holiday we went skiing and snowboarding. I am also flying regularly; you know my background as a pilot makes me take every opportunity to be airborne.
>
> I know that these great experiences would never have happened for me and my family if we had not worked together. By the way, on a less important note, our business has evolved tremendously. We are growing and expanding with the systems in place for our future success.
>
> *Entrepreneurial business group member, 2007*

Three Stages for Behavior Modification

Change is a reaction that requires us to adapt after the fact to something we have no control over. Just when we think we have our systems on go, change often requires us to re-examine and start all over again. Research indicates that change is one of the things humans fear and resist most.

The second stage is a shift. A shift is a change that is made internally. In making a shift, a person may respond differently in a similar situation from that point forward. So a shift can trigger an ongoing change in perspective. It may take some time to make the complete shift, but once it is made, it usually remains intact.

The third stage is an epiphany, a real transformational leap. Leaps are those "aha" moments where reality changes instantaneously. It is like an epiphany where in one minute reality is one thing and the next minute it has completely changed. It is powerful and permanent.

I experienced a leap when my husband and I met with a child psychologist who specialized in children with learning disabilities. Our son was seven years old and an amazingly bright boy who was struggling with reading. He could design incredibly intricate structures and figure out how machines worked but continued to lag behind in reading in the second grade.

The doctor asked my husband and me to make a list of things we would change about our son. Steve, my husband, said immediately, "Oh! I don't know anything I would change about Casey." I had been sitting there listing all the changes I wished could be made. When I heard my husband, I suddenly had an epiphany. I realized that I was not accepting my son as he was, and that moment changed my relationship with Casey forever. Dealing with his dyslexia became simply a process that had nothing to do with the extraordinary wonderful boy he was. I never again wished to change him! That leap was an amazing moment in my life.

Group coaching can allow participants to have those incredible moments of change and growth. It puts us in position to hear someone else say something that opens up an entirely different perspective. Often in a coaching group, as a group member is being coached, one or more of the other members have that moment of awareness that causes them to see their own situation from an entirely different vantage point.

One financial planner in a group explained to me and the other members of her group that she knew she had the expertise and knowledge to be a fine financial planner but that her lack of skill in prospecting limited her ability to build the successful business she wanted.

Her group members challenged her on this presumption on her part. In a round-robin, where all these financial professionals gave her feedback, she acknowledged that she didn't prospect for new clients for fear she would be rejected. The entire group shared their own fears and stories of rejection and how they had overcome this hurdle in their business. They assured her that she had a natural ability to connect and inspire others, and that all she needed to do was step out of her comfort zone and start connecting with more people.

Her group encouraged her to set a "stretch goal" for two weeks to prospect every day for at least an hour. She committed to the group to accept the challenge and follow through. When she checked in at the next meeting, she shared her most unlikely story of talking to a fellow driver at a gas station and handing him her card. Later in the week, he called to make an appointment for himself and his wife to come to her office to talk about life insurance.

One group member was very impressed and commented on the call, "Jan, you are such a great prospector that clients must come to you like bees to honey." Just that phrase caused her to make a shift in her thinking about prospecting, and over the next year, she learned to see herself as a really good prospector.

She related how the support of her group had given her the courage to step through her fears so that she would never fail to prospect and build her business again. Eight years later, when I spoke to a board of directors of a national financial association, she was one of the directors. It was wonderful to reconnect with her and hear her laugh and relate how her coaching group had been instrumental in helping her develop as a person and as a financial professional. She now has outstanding career success. She said that the shift in perspective about prospecting had been a catalyst that propelled her practice forward. Jan said that instead of being a problem, prospecting had become a real strength of hers.

Metaphors and similes are invaluable tools to help group members raise their level of awareness and shift perspectives. One of my favorite analogies that I use with groups is one I heard in a radio interview. I was driving when I heard this on a sports radio station. I was so afraid I would forget it that I drove off the highway, stopped, and wrote it down immediately.

Do You Trust Your Game?

Johnny Miller, the golf analyst, informed the television audience that golfer Ernie Ells trusted his game. His "color analyst" asked how he could tell that Ells trusted his game. Miller said that when you trust your game, you look where you want to go. When you don't trust your game, you look where you don't want to go, and where you look is where you end up.

Wow! Where you look is where you end up. This is an analogy I use to encourage group members to understand how important it is to be clear about what you want and keep your focus where you want to end up. That metaphor has become a powerful tool for creating awareness for my clients individually and in groups.

As the group coach, you can help clients with their awareness and in shifting their perspective by collecting and using metaphors and similes. Start by being aware of the metaphors you naturally use and the ones you hear from others around you. For example, the author Barbara Kingsolver wrote, "The very least you can do in your life is to figure out what you hope for. And the most you can do is live inside that hope. Not admire it from a distance, but live right in it, under its roof. Right now I'm living in that hope, running down its hallway, and touching the walls on both sides."

Creating awareness for group members can come from being coached individually or as a part of the natural process of group dynamics by the experience of being coached as part of another group members' coaching experience. Besides metaphors and similes, coaches use discovering, messaging, powerful questioning, and exploration as they help clients create awareness and shift perspectives.

Case Study: Role Playing to Create Awareness and Shift Perspectives

FRANK is a veterinary communication workshop sponsored by Pfizer Animal Health. A key component of a FRANK workshop involves breaking into small groups of five attendees per coach. The coach helps group members establish the coaching agreement with the small group participants by reinforcing the confidentiality of the events within the small group and establishing safe ground rules. The coach and the attendees observe the interaction of a veterinarian with a simulated client (SC). The simulated client is an actor who has been thoroughly trained in a real veterinary case. The veterinarian will set personal objectives for their learning session with the coach as their personal coaching agreement.

The attendees are assigned parts of the interview to observe carefully so they can provide feedback. Their feedback should also reflect the objectives the veterinarian has set for this role play. The coach or the veterinarian can call a time-out if the veterinarian is getting off course, or they can use it to point out an excellent example of a communication skill. The SC is able to "rewind" to a specific requested point and replay the interview. Once the time is up for the interaction, the attendees return to the room where the coach facilitates feedback from the veterinarian, the small group, the coach, and the SC. The entire interaction and the feedback session are recorded so the participants can go home and review their interaction and feedback visually. Each attendee participates in two different interactions with an SC over two days.

A participant who was in my assigned group came up to me and explained that she would not participate in a case. She was intimidated by the camera and the fact that others were observing her. She was almost in a state of panic. I asked her if she would at least come and participate in the feedback session because her perspective and feedback would be a gift to her colleagues. I assured her that she would not have to participate in a case if she chose to not participate.

The attendee decided to come to her small group. When she drew a case that was a hedgehog medicine case, she once again became very agitated and stated repeatedly that she knew nothing about hedgehogs. I calmly reminded her that the objective was to work on communication skills, and it was not about the medicine skills. This attendee performed such an outstanding job of communicating with her small group that all of us were literally sitting with our mouths open. She did an amazing job of asking powerful, open-ended questions. The comment from the small group during feedback time was that this was the best interaction they had ever experienced with a hedgehog case. This is an excellent example of taking away the participant's comfort level, allowing them to focus on their communication skills with an excellent outcome. This woman did not have her medical knowledge to revert to during the group interaction.

This was an important lesson for me as a coach and as a leader on the FRANK team. Setting proper expectations is important to gain participation by the small group members. It also illustrated to me that each and every case is relevant for the attendees regardless of their area of interest in veterinary medicine they practice. It truly is about the interactive communication and not about the medicine in this learning workshop and the following coaching sessions.

Feedback on the FRANK workshop has been very positive. The comments are that the small group coaching and the interactions with the SCs are the most valuable aspect of the workshops.

Coaching is valuable and can be applied in so many areas. This is a unique area that is making a difference in veterinary medicine.

Teresa M. Himebaugh, DVM
Senior Manager, USVS
South Central Region
teresa.himebaugh@pfizer.com

Coaching Questions:
1. Are you aware of every opportunity to coach group members in creating awareness?
2. Do you collect metaphors and similes that will be relevant and meaningful in your coaching groups?
3. How do you identify the important issues for creating change within the group?
4. What is each group member's role in creating awareness for others?
5. Name three ways you facilitate change, shifts, and leaps with group clients.

Chapter Thirteen
Eliminating Energy Drains

"In building a statue, a sculptor doesn't keep adding clay to his subject. He keeps chiseling away at the inessentials until the truth of its creation is revealed without obstructions."
—Bruce Lee, actor

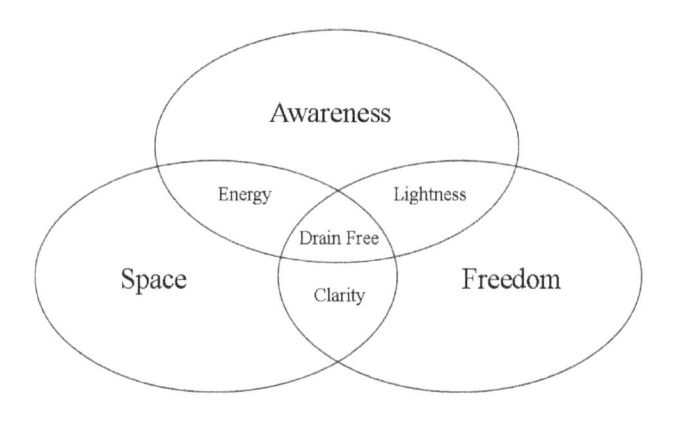

```
        Awareness
   Energy    Lightness
       Drain Free
  Space           Freedom
        Clarity
```

Energy Drains in Coaching Groups

Clarifying what you and your group members identify as energy drains is an important process that can improve the environment in a coaching group and make the experience more enjoyable. What is an energy drain for one person may not be for another, so this means raising your awareness as the coach of the group. Situations that create energy drains are a constantly recurring theme in coaching, partly because they are a constantly recurring phenomenon. Stacks of paper regenerate, spiders spin more webs, chores and errands have to be done again and again, boundary-invading people continue to try to invade, and every energy drain can reduce the value of the experience.

A financial professional who was a member of a coaching group shared with the group an energy drain that was affecting her feelings about going to work in her office regularly. She said that she brought a Dr. Pepper to work with her most days to put in the refrigerator and that a couple of days a week, when she went to the break room to relax, her Dr. Pepper was gone. She said no one would acknowledge that they took her cola. Because of her frustration, she started feeling mistrustful about the staff and the other financial representatives in the office. She said, "I am suspicious of everyone now and feel negative about the office in general."

I stepped in and asked her if I could do some laser coaching in the group. She agreed immediately, and I asked her a question, "What could you do that would prevent anyone from ever taking your Dr. Pepper again?" She thought about it and did some brainstorming with her group.

After all the input, she decided to write a message on a piece of paper that said, "This is Alice's Dr. Pepper, do not take it." She attached it to the can each day with a rubber band and waited to see the results. During the two weeks between the group call, no one had taken her cola. Her energy drain was eliminated. In the group meeting, she related how this situation in her office had affected her. She dreaded walking into the office, her relationships in the office had deteriorated, and her love for going to work was affected. With support of the group and being proactive, this energy drain was eliminated permanently. Even a small toleration can affect performance, attitude, and energy.

As you build and expand your group coaching business, you want to make sure that coaching multiple people in groups is something that brings energy, pleasure, and satisfaction into your business. The way to do that is put systems in place to have that occur easily. So getting clarity on what is an energy drain for you and what frees up your energy is a catalyst for putting systems in place that makes coaching multiple groups fun and enjoyable.

You may have an ability to cope and adjust to problems and frustrations and not truly recognize how much energy you expend in dealing with them. The only way you can discover whether or not that situation is an energy drain is to eliminate the toleration as an experiment and then be aware of how you feel once it is gone. If you feel lighter and more relaxed when you have eliminated the toleration, then it was indeed an energy drain and you will want to design a system to prevent it from reoccurring. If, on the other hand, you feel that you have lost something important by removing the toleration, then perhaps it is an important piece of how you choose to live your life and, for you, an energy generator.

Eliminating Energy Drains in My Office

Twelve years ago, I had stacks of paper all over my office along with books and magazine articles I was saving to read later. When I complained to a good friend and business associate who is a psychologist, he asked me when I would like to get rid of my clutter. My first thought was, *I know this is completely impossible*, but I answered, "Now!"

My friend came over to my office and checked it out. Then he asked how much time it would take to eliminate all the stacks. I went straight to feeling overwhelmed! I told him, "It will take me forever."

He looked amazed and mumbled, "Forever?"

I jumped in with, "Maybe not forever, but it would take a really long time." He asked if I could do it in a month. I thought, *If I worked on it all day every day, it surely wouldn't take a month.*

He persisted in asking me to give him a time frame. "Well," I answered, "it would probably take three days if I worked morning until night." He asked me how soon I could set aside three days.

I committed to doing it in two weeks and took a Friday and a weekend and tossed, filed, and scanned documents and articles. I put the books I needed in a new cabinet and gave the others away. It was wonderful! It was marvelous! I could see the tops of everything. I polished and shined my beautiful desk and my oak library table. I couldn't wait to tell my friend how great it was.

When I called him to report on my success, he congratulated me and asked how much it was worth to me to keep it that way. I said that I knew it was worth a lot to me, but I was so busy I didn't know if I had the time to keep it so spiffy. He asked if it was worth twenty minutes a day. "Only twenty minutes a day?" I asked. "Really?"

He said that if I filed and straightened before I left the office every day, twenty minutes was probably more than enough time. He thought I could probably do it in fifteen minutes. I had an epiphany. I suddenly had a neat and organized office that I had the time to maintain. It has become my standard to straighten my office each day before I leave. I often tell clients I can find anything in my office in thirty seconds. The payoff is that I smile every morning when I walk into my office and keep fresh flowers as a celebration for creating a beautiful working environment. One of my top business criteria is to maintain a neat and organized office.

Managing Energy Drains in the Group

So how will you manage and eliminate energy drains in your groups? I have had coaches in audiences ask me what to do about frustrating group coaching situations, and I have collected some of these over the years. Some of the questions and answers that follow may be helpful to you.

What if a group member wants to leave a group?

Typically this is handled in laser, one-on-one coaching, versus having a conversation with the entire group. It is important to actively listen to the person and make sure to clarify what the situation with that person is. Often it is a reaction to a situation that causes them to be temporarily frustrated or something that can be talked through and remedied.

Asking permission to explore the group member's reaction is a good strategy for the group coach. That may lead to what is working and what is not working for that person in the group. It is a good opportunity to be the champion for the group member. Take the time to point out the value that person has brought to the group and to give examples of how that value has impacted others. One of the problems may be that this person is disappointed because of his or her performance and the feeling that he or she has not stepped up to the commitments of the group. The most common result in this situation will be that the group member's concerns can be remedied and he or she can return to the group more actively engaged than before. Some special time in laser coaching with the person can help them refocus and get back on track.

If the person does leave the group, this may provide the opportunity to help them design an exit strategy that will make them feel "whole" (honored and valued) and allow them to leave in a way that the group will understand and hopefully accept graciously. Handled gracefully, this can be a positive experience for everyone.

It is important for the coach to maintain coaching ethics and honor the confidentiality of the coaching relationship for the exiting group member. As part of the exit strategy, it is important to have an agreement with the exiting group member on what can be shared with the rest of the group. Encouraging that person to share a message by e-mail or in person may serve everyone concerned best. If the coach delivers the message, it is important to share a message that is both honest and honoring everyone involved.

What if most everyone wants to leave the group?

There are a couple of options in that case. If everyone wants to leave the group, it is obvious the group that is not meeting the needs of the group members. This may be an opportunity to do a survey, distribute a questionnaire, and reorganize the group with a new mission or purpose. It is important to consider that the group may have served the purpose it was created for. Ask the group if it is time to have a graduation ceremony and celebrate the value the group has brought to each of the members. That is a lovely way to complete the group process.

One company coaching group that had been together two years seemed to be coming to an end. The group members were sharing e-mails that suggested the group was no longer meeting some members' expectations. I surrendered any leadership on my part and left the decision solely to them. I asked them to decide whether or not to continue and stated that they would have to create the mission, purpose, and agenda for the group if the decision was to continue. I supplied them with several documents to help them through the process, including one that Thomas Leonard had created, called "101 Things to Work on With a Coach."

The group met on a bridge line without me in attendance and came back with a proposed six-month plan. They said the agenda for the next six months was for each member to rotate being in charge of creating agendas. They took the "101 Things to Work on With a Coach" and designated dates for each member to be in charge of the agenda for a specific call. That member would choose a topic from that list and then not share the topic with me until we had all joined the call. This plan was a little scary for me because I didn't have a chance to prepare for the calls at all, but it was definitely exciting and a challenge for me as their coach, and they were delighted that I had accepted the challenge. The group continued on for another year. The result was that we all enjoyed the fact that they had "pulled off" a coup and were all fired up about the group again.

Being willing to experiment and step away and trust the group saved the group and created immense value for each group member and for me as the coach. It definitely made them closer as a group and inspired them to realize that they could create exactly what they wanted. As the group continued that next year, they spoke up if they weren't pleased with what was happening and were emboldened, knowing they had the power to change what wasn't working. They truly owned their own group.

What if someone in the group talks all the time?
A real energy drain in groups is when a group member talks to the exclusion of others. This is a significant problem, which can cause members to disengage or not show up for the call. It is the group coach's job to

recognize this problem and act quickly to correct it. One of the most effective ways to handle this is to address the issue in the guidelines for the group.

An effective guideline for managing the member who talks too much is introducing laser speak. This is so important a topic that there is an entire chapter in this book on the subject. If laser speak is a standard in your groups, then the group will start reminding members immediately that laser speak is the rule. The advantage for the coach is that it is not necessary for the coach to monitor the member's behavior. When group members can monitor and prevent long monologues, the quicker this behavior will cease to be a problem.

What if someone won't talk or contribute?

One of the reasons we collect a portfolio at the beginning that includes all the members of a group is so that I have information to help when situations like this occur. Each member answers the "Thoughtful Questions." These questions explore the reasons why a group member is joining the group, along with how they can contribute, as well as what they want to receive from the group. When someone is not stepping up in the group and sharing with the other group members, I go back to those initial thoughtful questions and ferret out what is important to that person and what they can bring to the group. Then, in laser coaching and in the group, I encourage that person to reassess what their goal is about receiving in the group and exploring how he or she might contribute more. I also encourage group members to work with a sponsor or mentor in the company, if possible, to have a team approach to encouraging the person to contribute and connect in the group.

What happens if people don't keep their commitments?

I ask each group member what their commitment to the group is for the next two weeks. It is critical that I do not ask a member to commit to me as their coach but to commit to the group. When the group is a formed group, everyone counts on the completion of those commitments. It is a great opportunity for accountability, because group members who are keeping their commitments will challenge those who are not. It is amazing what that peer pressure will do. Where a client might make an excuse to a coach, they will work really hard to carry out the commitment to the group. In that circumstance, I have seen a group member work late and over the weekend to honor their commitment so they don't have to acknowledge they didn't do what they said they would.

What happens if there is a rift in the group or if some people get along and connect and others don't?
All of my groups are on the phone, and none of the group members have ever worked together before they joined the group. By creating a coaching environment where all the group members are honored and championed by the coach and everyone is given the opportunity to share and interact in a coach-like manner with others, I have had very little problems with rifts or misunderstandings. Keeping that "clear water" is important. That means that as a group coach, I am not stepping over anything. If someone is feeling uncomfortable or unhappy or frustrated or upset, I can usually sense that as his or her coach. This is typically intuitive and predicated by what they say or don't say or the way they disappear or sigh or complain, or challenge inappropriately during a group meeting. If I am feeling some angst in the group, there almost always is a problem. I step in and ask, "I am feeling like there is some tension and frustration in the group. Am I the only one who is experiencing this? Who can offer some insight to the meeting today?" By addressing it immediately, it becomes much easier to resolve than to let it fester for a few weeks.

What do I do if I ask permission and someone won't give it to me?
My number one rule is that "no" is as acceptable an answer from a group member as "yes" is. If I ask someone if I can coach him or her in the group and that person says no, then I assume they have a very good reason for that answer. I then move to another person, without feeling any energy about the person who said no. That freedom to respond honestly in the group is a key component in having the group move to being a formed group. If there is a "no" from someone in the group, there is typically someone in the group who can be counted on to step up and participate fully, so the energy in the call returns quickly. If no one steps up, the coach can use a group coaching story or move on to something that is relevant to the group.

What do I do if I ask for agenda items and no one contributes anything?
I always have some agenda items in reserve because of the thoughtful questions. I return to the skills and tools they want to improve upon that they shared in the beginning of the group. I also make notes during the group meetings and note things that are relevant that we haven't had the time to address. I also have resources from the program outline or from former groups. I don't feel there is a lack of agenda items, but I do encourage them to share "just in time" concerns or opportunities even as we are gathering for the group call. It is often those last-minute items that

can turn an ordinary call into an exceptional group meeting. The key is for everyone to be flexible and on board with changing the agenda at the last minute. The real answer to the question is to keep asking and making sure the agenda is fluid enough to add new agenda items at the last minute.

What do I do if I ask for agenda items and they are all different?
It almost never happens that everyone has a pressing agenda item! However, if there are several agenda items and I am not certain we have adequate time to address them all, an e-mail to the group with a ranking form is a good solution. I ask them to rank agenda items on a scale of one to five in importance, and then the group makes the decision about what would be most meaningful to them. Also, some agenda items may be more time sensitive than others, so taking that into consideration is important. The key is to have buy-in from the group so that they decide and agree on any agenda changes or additions. If someone wants to add an agenda item after the group starts, then the group members discuss the relevance of the item and make recommendations. Often, after discussion, someone will say something like, "Since this isn't that relevant for most of us, why don't you take this off-line and laser coach with Jerry individually?"

I'm afraid to coach someone in front of the group. How do I get comfortable coaching in public?
I now know I can let go of the outcome. Coaching is not a seamless process; it is a real interaction. I remember watching Laura Berman Fortgang coaching before a crowd of coaches and potential coaches here in Dallas. She invited someone in the audience to volunteer for coaching. It wasn't long before it was obvious that the issue the person was dealing with was not appropriate for the demonstration and that the coaching was becoming bogged down with details.

I loved how quickly and effectively Laura exited the coaching demonstration. She said that she felt this issue was something that would take more time than was allotted for in the demo. She asked the person to give her his card and asked if it was okay for them to set up an appointment for a coaching session after the presentation so they could follow through on a one-on-one basis. He agreed and brought his card up to the stage. Laura then asked if there was someone who had an issue that could be addressed and dealt with quickly without a lot of background info. Someone raised her hand quickly, and Laura moved forward with a very effective coaching demonstration. Once I experienced this exit strategy, I have never been uneasy about coaching in public. I know now that I do not have to be caught in a coaching session that is going nowhere. I can exit graciously and move to a more productive demonstration.

What happens if people move toward their goals at different rates, so someone is moving fast and someone else is moving really slowly?
As the coach of the group as well as the individuals in the group, it is my job to champion everyone. The fast starters can be highlighted to encourage others. Those in the middle of the pack can be encouraged by highlighting what is working well for them and encouraging more of those "bright spots." Those who are not moving forward can receive some special attention with laser coaching or with a sponsor or mentor from the company. As the coach, I can ask for encouragement for that person from their entire group. It is amazing what slow starters can achieve once their momentum and success start to build.

What happens if someone frequently misses the group meetings?
This can cause frustration and concern, especially in a formed group. After a group forms, it is not always the coach's responsibility to deal with this situation. The group members generally step up and encourage the member to participate regularly, and they often challenge them if they don't. In a formed group, members typically call in or join in even when they are on vacation. Group members have called in from the beach in Hawaii and halfway up a mountain in the Rockies.

What do you do if you slip and there is a break in integrity?
What if you don't send a follow-up as promised, forget to ask permission, send the wrong file out, or are rude or judgmental in the group? Everyone makes mistakes, including professional coaches. I use the apology process when I make a mistake and want to communicate the situation to a group. I acknowledge what I have done and apologize for it. The next step is to ask what I can do to make amends, and then I tell the person how much their relationship means to me and promise not to make that mistake again. Instead of just saying I'm sorry, this process is very effective in changing the energy in the group and helps retain good relationships.

What do I do if I need to raise the price of the group?
You have the option of raising the price for your groups anytime you start a new group of individuals or company groups. Once you have started a group with an agreed-upon price structure, you do not have the option to change it unless everyone in the group agrees. There is no reason a pricing

conversation can't take place in the group and an agreement reached. The most important thing is that you are transparent with all the group members.

What do I do if group members find out that they're paying different rates?

I let people know that I will be giving a few scholarships for specific reasons and that they will get a price break if they bring another person into the group or refer someone who joins a group. Those are the only circumstances that I change rates, unless I make that rate available to everyone. If you are open about your agreements, there is no need to be concerned about why some people may be paying more than others. They will all know the parameters and the exceptions. If you are regularly coaching groups, there will be things that will go wrong and as a result create an energy drain for you and your group members. As a tolerations eliminator, you will want to remove as many of these drains as possible.

It's not clear why we put up with problems, energy drainers, uncomfortable situations, and frustrations; but the fact is that we tolerate far more than is healthy or smart. We can even feel proud that we are good at coping, handling, accepting, dealing with, and solving that we get used to the problems and we may even define ourselves as a "problem solver." If you make the switch from being a "problem solver" to becoming a "problem eliminator," you may increase the joy and the energy in your life. Give it a try!

Case Study—Larry Ousley, PCC

Magic happens when a person participates in a coaching group. Participants often have breakthroughs. Individual coaching aids the client in clarifying their intentions, focusing on them, and finding patterns of ease and flow in their life. Group coaching, when guided by a skilled group coach, brings the added dimension of greater inspiration and support for transformation through the additional relationships in the group. As I have led coaching groups, I've seen people make progress in areas of their lives in which they have been "tolerating" frustration of their aspirations for years.

One dramatic example occurred a few years ago in a group of clergy that I coached. Clergy, as busy professionals, often end up neglecting their needs as they minister to the needs of others. How were these clergy going to get "unstuck" from ruts that were restricting them? Being in this coaching group with others who have similar roles and lifestyles made a huge difference in breaking the inertia pattern that was limiting everyone in the group. The particular group was part of a larger program called Covenant Coaching Circles.

The area where the group really found traction was on the issue of self-care. It seems strange in a way that ordained ministers who are all about inviting persons to live a whole life of being in love with God and contributing to the well-being of others would have trouble caring for the temple of their own bodies in order to be vital and effective in their lives and ministry.

After awhile it became clear that a common theme for the group was their tolerating unrealistic expectations from parishioners about aspects of the clergy's ministry or lives. The expectations became internalized so that the pressure was mostly from within group members' own heads. Structuring a balanced approach to living and ministry within the supportive community of the coaching group, which brought in the additional factor of peer support and encouragement, made all the difference.

Declaring their goals in the midst of the group in the area of self-care enabled the participants to follow through more effectively. Further, being coached in the presence and sometimes with the aid of other group members helped the clergy to make progress. Thus, unrealistic pressure experienced by each group member, both from the outside and the inside, was lessened. Further, group members were more likely to face issues of lack of wholeness and intentionality that they had been tolerating in their lives for years.

Larry Ousley, PCC
Sacred Fire Coaching
Executive Director, Intentional Growth Center and Composing Your Life
Larry@LarryOusley.com

Group coaching offers many benefits. One significant benefit is to help coaches lessen what they are tolerating within their coaching business and in their lives to create the time and space to coach groups.

Coaching Questions:

1. What is it that would drain your energy around managing multiple groups?
2. Can you delegate that aspect of your group coaching model?
3. How can you streamline managing your individual and client information?
4. How will you manage the multiple emails and messages you receive?
5. Can you list six key things that need to be eliminate in order to coach groups?

Chapter Fourteen
Return on Investment

"We are taking significant steps to reduce our cost structure and sharpen our focus on the services that hold the best potential for growth and return on investment."
—William Esrey, Chairman Emeritus of Sprint Corporation

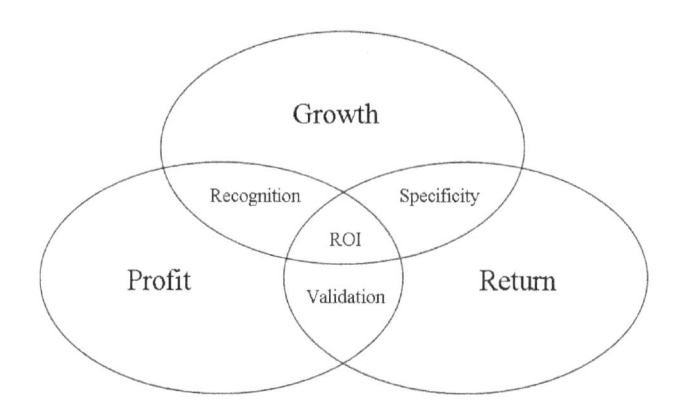

Coaching is a rapidly growing 2.5-billion-dollar service industry embraced by many of the Fortune 500 corporations globally and hundreds of smaller companies and organizations. As more scalable solutions for promoting individual growth and development are being demanded in the marketplace, elevating your coaching skills and embracing group coaching can leverage and expand your own coaching offerings resulting in a strong return on investment both for you as a coach and for the organizations where you coach groups.

Return on Investment (ROI)

The return on investment is the measure of the financial gain (or loss) of a project in relation to its cost. In order to effectively integrate and expand the reach of group coaching with individuals, companies, and organizations, it is important to identify the results wanted from a group coaching initiative and to be able to measure the return on investment based on the target deliverables. More people can be coached in a shorter period of time and for a lower cost. Quantifying how scalable and effective group coaching is the purpose of measuring group coaching ROI.

Why is ROI Relevant?
- ROI is relevant when quantifying of the effectiveness of group coaching. Companies and organizations are willing to invest time and money in group coaching if they have ROI that shows valuable results.
- Determining ROI measurements ensures that the company, the participants, and the group coach will begin the group coaching project clear about the results expected and track those results along the way.
- ROI provides a commonly accepted data reported on the measures stipulated.
- Measuring ROI helps add to the growing data about the overall effectiveness of coaching.

Examples of Return on Investment Data Collection

1. The Manchester Executive Coaching Survey is believed to be the first major study to quantify the business impact of executive coaching. It found that participating companies who provided coaching to its executives realized an average return on investment (ROI) of almost six times the cost of the coaching.
http://www.coachfederation.org

2. The Sales Executive Council Research on Coaching in Corporations also showed a high ROI for coaching and has caught the attention of corporate decision makers.
www.coachfederation.org/**research**

3. Executive Recruiter News reports that executive coaching delivers an ROI of almost six times the initial cost of coaching. Seventy percent of executives who participated in the Right's Management Consultants survey claim that their ROI was at least one hundred thousand dollars, and another 30 % put their ROI between five hundred thousand and one million dollars. Joy McGovern,

Senior VP and Managing Consultant of Right's Organizational Consulting Practice says, "The survey results corroborate what coaching participants and first-hand observers have seen, that coaching can have a dramatic impact on change in executive behavior and organizational improvements." Resource: The International Coach Federation (IFC) www.coachfederation.org/**research**

4. ICF helps quantify the value of coaching by evaluating coaching results worldwide in order to give the International PRISM award to the most outstanding companies using professional coaching. Many local ICF chapters give their own PRISM award to a local company or organization.

Key to Developing ROI for Group Coaching

1. In order for a ROI result to be meaningful, it must be measurable. Identify what's meaningful to the stakeholders, the company, the organization, and the participants. Require an agreement at the beginning of the coaching engagement to collect the data necessary for tracking ROI.
2. Set up a system for measuring ROI.
3. Measuring and collecting data should not be done by the coach. If there is a system for tracking specific deliverables internally in a company, the company can measure and record results. Production numbers, retention, and high potential candidate promotions are typical ROI measurable outcomes.

Measurable results do not have to be completely objective. Soft skill measures can also be quantified, such as:

1. Client satisfaction
2. Employee satisfaction and retention
3. Leadership effectiveness
4. Besides the company's method of measuring, coaches can collect data from participants in a group coaching experience via surveys, questionnaires, and interviews.

Measurable results that are tied directly to an organization's top initiatives are extremely valuable and compelling. Increased production and retention of high producers are vital to companies in today's marketplace. Showing a favorable ROI with regard to these measures allows companies and organizations to make knowledge-based decisions about buying group coaching.

Involve the group members by clearly and comprehensively defining the most important results that can actually be achieved for them individually, collectively commit to those results, and co-create the group agenda to support them. Then track and measure the process and progress from the actual participants.

Key Measurements in Developing the ROI for Group Coaching

Keep sustainability in mind when developing your group coaching ROI. In order for the measurables to be meaningful in the long term, the results must be sustainable.

Examples:
1. Percentage of increase in production over three years.
2. Increase in sales on a quarterly basis.
3. Percentage of increase in employee retention based on yearly numbers.
4. Increase in recruitment numbers.
5. Increase in group members' satisfaction within their company.
6. Improvement in group members' communication effectiveness.
7. Increase in group members' leadership effectiveness.
8. Improvement in teamwork.
    a. At the executive level
    b. In company terms
9. Improvement in the availability and effectiveness of the appropriate system.

Client Example of ROI

A testimonial for learning and developing with group coaching
Coach James Caplin, PCC in the UK
Company-Based ROI Collection Methods

The group coaching has had outstanding results. People in the business are commenting on the significant improvements that the people in this group have achieved.

We have learned a lot from each other and have learned to value each other's experience, insights, and observations. Having the variety of opinions, insights, and challenges has made this a unique experience that has provoked deep thoughts and significant changes. You could call it raft building with only the mind as a resource. We have managed to cross the lake successfully and are looking forward to new challenges.

The group coaching experience has also enabled a number of individuals to launch into individual coaching in a seamless and committed way that has really got the most from the opportunity. Goals for these people have been clearer and larger; commitment to the process has been stronger and more committed.

All of this will further improve the effectiveness of my people in the business and has changed us in profound and significant ways.

At times the effort each person in the group is putting in can vary, and it has been very important for us to challenge each other on our commitment to the work involved in trying to deliver these improvements. It is not always easy to find time. We must remain committed to the specific challenge we set ourselves and review if we are making good enough progress in order to recommit and move on.

To change the opinions of colleagues to each other, after five to ten years of working with each other is truly difficult. This has happened as a result of the improvements the coaching has delivered to the people and to our business, and it clearly shows.

Tom Barnard, Director Projects, Process, and IT DaimlerChrysler Services UK Limited

Companies are typically already measuring ROI data, so there may already be a tracking system in place that your program can tap into. What is important is to get a benchmark established before the group coaching program is launched to determine what percent increase in profit, productivity, and retention would be a fair and reasonable goal to set for the project. Companies are likely already tracking numbers on employee production, department, and division sales numbers, employee retention data, recruitment numbers, and customer satisfaction.

When you are negotiating with a company that has an existing measurement system, you can encourage them as they collect the data to provide you with not only the established base numbers, but also periodic updates throughout the coaching engagement. This allows you to be updated regularly so you can evaluate what is working well and where some shift of focus and upgrade may be needed. The important thing is that the information is shared with the participants in the initiative. As participants own their group, they will provide incredible input and recommendations for raising the bar and inspiring more involvement and opportunity.

In addition, if new measurements are relevant, they can be created to assess the effect of coaching on other issues: employee satisfaction, team communication efficiency, high potential leadership advancement, improvement in teamwork, and executive peer group effectiveness are examples.

Often the group coach has the opportunity to provide measurement tools, surveys, polls, and testimonials as part of the ROI conversations.

I am providing an example of a ROI measurement tool developed by an outstanding group coach who works with entrepreneurial companies. The following is an example of a ROI measurement tool that is a two-part questionnaire developed by group coach Bud Roth.

Part one is completed electronically via e-mail and examines group members' initial reaction to coaching, what they've learned, and how they've applied what they learned. It captures their initial assessment of the business impact.

Part two is conducted in the form of a telephone interview conducted privately between the group member and the person conducting the measurement for the company. The coach does not do this. This interview probes deeper into personal satisfaction, business impact, and the financial return on investment.

{Add Your Company Name}
Group Coaching Payback Analysis

Please complete the attached analysis as best you can. We are seeking methods to measure the return on investment of the group coaching process. You may have some suggestions to modify the format to generate an accurate assessment. We encourage the client to identify their desired outcomes and use their measuring process to validate their payback from coaching. The form below is best completed by hand after printing it out.

We know that there are many intangible benefits to coaching, like human relations, customer satisfaction, and communications. Although the intangible benefits eventually impact the bottom line, it remains important to measure the payback in dollars or percents of increased performance. Our intention is to build a solid business case to support group coaching as one of the most effective development methods that create substantial value to the enterprise. The time for review and analysis will help this effort.

The group must first decide if the form will be completed for the entire group or for each individual. If the outcomes are focused on the entire group, complete one form. If the outcomes are for individual growth and development, each individual needs to complete a form. Of course, you can complete the form both ways if you wish. There is also an optional, open-ended measurement form included.

At this time just complete the far left column of the form. Add or subtract from the list of competencies (attributes) to suit your interests. After we have completed the group coaching process, I will ask you to complete the remainder of the format. The idea is for you to self identify where you know or think you currently fall on this ten-point scale at the beginning of your coaching experience. Later, of course, you will measure the change, if any, for each of the competencies. At that time we will apply dollars to the tangible gains and a percentage of improvements to the intangibles. Although this measurement method is somewhat subjective, it will describe the payback and value of group coaching. Also, identify other factors outside of the coaching experience that may have influenced the results.

Thank you for your participation. Return the form to me quickly. Please call me with any questions or comments.

Regards, Bud Roth

Case Study from Bud Roth

Client: Privately held, three-year-old communications and printing company with 125 people. Growing by acquisition of small related companies and an aggressive sales force. Leadership development and change management is needed for growth and sustainability.

Situation: The company has a good reputation within the state and is considered a very successful printer within their industry. Employee satisfaction surveys show a steady improvement over the past three years. Integrating the business cultures of the recently acquired companies is cumbersome and overwhelming. This culture is reactive, lacks accountability, and managers are not taking initiative. Leaders need to become business thinkers, build cohesive teams, and work cooperatively across functional lines. People are not collaborating effectively, sharing their knowledge, or learning from their mistakes. The organization is working in self-contained units with limited communication across boundaries, and everyone is overcommitted.

The Plan
- Assess the organization by interviewing individuals and groups of employees.
- Develop an action plan with the leadership teams to move forward.
- Create task teams to make operational changes for improving work flow.
- Group coaching for the executive and midmanagement leadership teams to include monthly private coaching for all leaders for individual development.
- Train leaders in coaching techniques.
- Measure the results over a nine-month period.

Execution of the Plan
- Interviewed individuals and groups of employees, wrote a report, and met with both leadership teams to develop the action plan.
- Created five task teams, facilitated the charter development and initial meetings.
- Administered a personal assessment with each leader, interpreted the results and had each person write their personal development plan. Private coaching occurred once a month for six months.

- Group coaching occurred with the executive team and midmanager leadership teams separately. Met two times each month as a group for six months, plus three months of monthly reinforcement meetings. The midmanagement group wanted to continue monthly meetings after the professional coach was not involved.
- Held a one-day, off-site training program to learn and practice coaching skills after three months of group and individual coaching. Participants were mentored on applying coaching skills over the next three months.
- Measured the progress with participants regularly and performed a ROI analysis of the impact of group coaching.

The Results
- Each leader expressed many anecdotal examples of the benefits of their own personal coaching experience. The executive team decided not to buy another company in 2006.
- The silos started breaking down and effective collaboration occurred. They all embraced healthy conflict in meetings. Problem resolutions were achieved faster.
- Task teams were stopped early on. Consequently, the process improvements had limited results.
- The ROI analysis revealed a $1.9 million productivity gain and a 22% improvement in leadership competencies.
- The company ended fiscal 2006 with a 38% sales increase; revenue increased $5.2 million to $19.5 million; profits increased to 25% from a year ago. (Industry profit average is 3%.)

Measure the Payback of Group Coaching
1. Current status or situation(s)
2. Desired outcomes from group coaching
3. Current client measures that may indicate a payback from group coaching
4. Agreed-upon outcomes from group coaching

Coach-Based ROI Collection Methods

Coaches can also regularly collect and measure the ROI of their group coaching outside of companies:
- Send out periodic questionnaires.
- Use the answers collected to assess and upgrade group effectiveness.

- Keep e-mails and testimonials from group members.
- Use correspondence from group members in quarterly or year-end reports as deliverables to the company (with your clients' permission).
- Get copies of the data that companies have collected.
- Use this to compile your own company's ROI statistics.

How Group Coaching Benefits Companies
1. Group coaching increases the scalability of coaching within a company or organization.
2. Coaching improves the retention rate for a company by creating happier, more productive employees.
3. Key employees often view coaching as a perk and an added value.
4. Group coaching is being used to recruit top candidates, as companies that provide group coaching are seen as a good place to work.
5. A recent study shows that participating in coaching creates more awareness of and focus on company initiatives, meaning company goals and initiatives are more likely to be achieved.

How Measuring ROI Benefits Companies
- Measuring ROI shows companies that group coaching is effective.
- ROI measurements can help recruitment efforts, because they show that the company is committed to an employee development program based on proven results.
- The ROI data demonstrates that employee professional development dollars go further and produce better results with the group coaching model.
- The production of individual employees can significantly increase when they are being coached in a group. Since the company is measuring this, they can pinpoint what factors contributed to their success and replicate this with other employees.

How Measuring ROI Benefits Participants
- Participants have access to specific data that shows their individual improvements, which can be used during performance reviews and promotion negotiations.
- Participants have a record of what worked for them and by how much, allowing them to better allocate their personal time and resources.

- When the ROI of a coaching group reflects positive results, it allows employees to lobby for continuing group coaching programs.

How Measuring ROI Benefits Coaches
- Measuring ROI creates data to verify the worth of group coaching when you market peer groups as a key piece of your offerings as a coach.
- ROI data helps the coach feel more confident when presenting peer coaching groups as an option to companies and organizations.
- The process involved in measuring ROI involves a variety of people in the company, which results in broadening and deepening the coach's reach and relevance in the organization.
- ROI data helps the coach decide how to best leverage his or her time to maximize their personal highest and best use of time and focus.
- ROI data can help a coach become more profitable by focusing on projects that yield a high return for the organization.

Good data spreads fast! High return on investment creates an internal buzz in an organization that encourages the expansion of group coaching.

Bud Roth, PCC
Roth Consulting Group, LCC
budroth@rothcg.com
www.rothcg.com

Coaching Questions:

1. Are you comfortable addressing return on investment as you market your coaching groups?
2. When negotiating with a company or organization about starting groups, do you address ROI as part of the conversation?
3. Will you have methods for collecting results with your groups and partner with the group members and the company or organization to assess and report on the results?
4. Are you comfortable with someone else collecting and assessing the value to the organization for the coaching groups?
5. How will you deliver the information on the return on investment to group members and the organization?

Chapter Fifteen
Marketing Group Coaching

"Pay any price to stay in the presence of extraordinary people."
—Mike Murdock

```
        ┌─────────────────┐
        │    Alliances    │
   ┌────┤                 ├────┐
   │    │   Visibility    │    │
   │    │  ┌───────────┐  │    │
   │    └──┤Successful ├──┘    │
   │       │ Marketing │       │
   │Specificity        │Experiments│
   │       │  Insight  │       │
   └───────┴───────────┴───────┘
```

Before you start marketing coaching groups, it is important that you have had an experience being a member of a coaching group. Besides the incredible wisdom of the group, there is a peer commitment and accountability that allows participants to achieve extraordinary results. Unless you have a peer group experience, it is difficult to effectively attract others into your groups. It was in the group experience that I developed the passion for creating groups and the desire to make them the centerpiece of my coaching business. Your personal experience is an essential part of developing as a group coach. You will also be able to collect personal success stories and testimonials that will help you explain what the group coaching experience is like. Once the value of the group experience has infused you, it makes attracting others to your groups much easier.

Another important step for a coach starting a group is developing a comfort level with the whole idea of marketing. For me, the idea of having a marketing plan and strategy sounded difficult and somewhat daunting. I had taken a marketing course at Colorado State University and had worked on a detailed and tedious marketing plan. I thought about my reaction to the concept of marketing and realized that it was important for me to reorient my thinking about marketing and identify a personal strength that I had that would help me create groups.

That strength was in the words "collecting community." All my life I have collected people in groups, teams, organizations, volunteer efforts, professional associations, and fun excursions. I love including as many people as possible in adventures. When I decided that instead of marketing groups, I would start collecting them, it was magical. That shift in language allowed me to enjoy the process of building coaching groups instead of dreading it.

What are your strengths that might conjure up your marketing words? What is a word that feels comfortable and inspiring for you? It could be market, attract, collect, create, assemble, invite, announce, accumulate, amass, gather, or bring together.

"If you have a dream you can do yourself, it's not a big enough dream."

—anon

Key Ways to Attract Clients

Create a research and development (R&D) team of your ideal clients to attract your first group. Let them know that they are designing a group that allows the members to achieve extraordinary results, then listen to their ideas and feedback about what they would want in the group. If they help you develop the program, they will join and bring others with them. Jim Vuocolo, MCC, uses this methodology to market his groups. One of his ideal clients is the attorney who is a solo practitioner. Jim invites clients and contacts in this category to join an R&D team, where they explore the topics and agendas they would find value improving and achieving with a coach and a group of seasoned peers in the profession. After they complete the process of creating their ideal group program, it is natural that they want to be a part of the group themselves. So the R&D team members made up the first group and then became advocates for later groups of lawyers.

Create excitement in your social network. A few strategies for launching your first group is to announce an exciting program designed specifically for your ideal clients, promote a book you have written or a favorite new book that could be transformational for your ideal clients, publish an article that is of specific interest and value and share it with all of your network, or create and promote a teleclass or a seminar especially if it provides continuing education hours for recertification for your ideal clients. By publishing a tips book, an e-book, a tape, or CD for your niche clients, you can create interest, revenue, and traffic to your website. You can also host a teleforum and ask your advocates to invite their network to be a part of this event. By being generous and sharing valuable resources with your clients and community at no cost to them, you also can grow your social capital and attract new clients.

Market group coaching to companies through your advocates. Besides asking your advocates for introductions to decision makers, it is important to collaborate with them to identify initiatives they need to implement and design and tailor coaching groups that will execute a program that can achieve the results they want. You can start the relationship with the company by offering a pilot program that will give the company and the group coaching participants a chance to experience the power and results coaching groups bring. The advocate can also help you in pricing and designing programs and reaching agreements with the company.

Form an alliance with your individual clients, colleagues, or advocates to offer seminars or workshops (informational or inspirational) that neither of you could offer alone but both of you can attract together. Coaches can join attorneys, accountants, financial planners, real estate professionals, and sales professionals to share amazing facilities and clients. These events can be either live events at conferences, regional meetings, association events, or they can be virtual events. This is value equals value for the participants, for the coach, and for the professional colleague. Everyone adds to their visibility and social capital.

Convert your individual clients into group clients and invite them to bring peers and colleagues with them. This can add incredible value to your individual client because they can maintain a coaching relationship with you while joining peers on their business or professional level and take advantage of their expertise and insights. By encouraging these clients to bring in other ideal clients to the group, they become advocates for you while you provide them the opportunity to join colleagues in the group experience. (Examples are sales reps into attraction groups, company managers into coaching proficiency groups, etc.)

Get visible—speak and make presentations. Create a visible presence with your ideal clients. Know the organizations your clients belong to, the publications they read, and the resources they look for—then show up in as many of those places as possible. (Examples are brown bag lunches, sales meetings, and professional development.) Start a PR kit that encourages you and gives credibility within your niche. Cooperate with other organizations to achieve name and brand recognition you could not achieve on your own. Target them in an e-mail newsletter.

One of the most effective methods of getting visible is to schedule teleforums on subjects of interest to your ideal clients. The key is to have an individual or group client who is interested and excited about helping you create more groups of professionals just like her or him. One advocate can help you create a marketing engine for creating future groups. My method of collaborating with an advocate includes the following steps:

- Share my vision of having valuable teleforums for financial professionals with two or three of my financial clients who are advocates.
- Ask these advocates to send out invitations to other financial professionals in their database who might be interested in relevant information and resources in their field. (Note: You are *not* asking your advocates to turn over their database of clients, colleagues, and friends to you. They will send out an invitation that you can help them write to people they choose).
- Invite the advocate or advocates to join the teleforum to greet their friends and colleagues and to participate in the conversation.
- During the course of the teleforum conversation, ask permission to coach someone. This allows everyone to experience what coaching in a group is like. With advocates on the call, there is no need to be uneasy that no one will step up to be coached, because your advocates have been alerted so they can step up if need be. Coaching someone live on the teleforum allows them to experience the value of coaching and the power of joining peers in the group experience.
- Share in the group two or three key points from a "Top Ten List" of valuable information on how to be a more effective leader, advisor, manager, or coach.

- As part of the presentation, discuss the value of being a part of a group that includes your own coach and a small group of outstanding peers. Encourage your advocates who are group members to share their personal experiences with everyone on the teleforum.
- At the end of the teleforum, offer to share the entire resource list with any attendee who sends you an e-mail requesting the "Top Ten" and reminding them that they will get an invitation to be a part of the next group. Once they contact you personally, their contact information can become part of your database.
- Along with the resources list, attendees will receive an invitation to join a coaching group. All the relevant information about cost, time, and dates will be included in this marketing piece.

Market to companies through your advocates to identify an initiative they have and tailor a coaching group that will help them achieve the results they want. Start the relationship by offering a pilot program that will give the company and the group coaching participants a chance to experience the power and results coaching groups bring. Co-design the proposal and the agreement with the internal advocate.

Example on Getting Started as a Group Coach in a Company
One of my favorite clients in 1997 was an executive in a financial services company. After coaching her for two years, her business had systems in place, she was delegating regularly, her employees were working as an effective team, and she had created time to take care of herself and enjoy her life. She always loved the business she was in; she was just frustrated that she had to work so hard without getting the results she felt capable of. After coaching, she was achieving at the highest level in her company.

She talked to me about what a great business financial service was for women and how many were leaving before they were there five years. She told me that she wished we could get coaching for women so that they could establish their businesses and create the lifestyle that she had. We brainstormed about how we could get the company to sponsor coaching. The cost of providing individual coaching for advisors was not feasible for the company, so we talked about putting the women in groups.

She flew from Seattle to the home office of the company in the Midwest and did a PowerPoint presentation before three key decision makers in the company and got the program approved. We did a year pilot program for women who had been in the business from three to five years. At the end of six months, the company asked me to send a report or deliverable to the company with testimonials from the participants and a recapitulating of the group members' production numbers, attendance, retention, and developmental progress. The most important result was that only one of the women who participated in the groups left the company.

The following year the program expanded to ten groups. The price point for the groups was a monthly fee per group. The groups met twice a month for one hour. Each group had from five to seven advisors as members. I coached groups in the company for five years, and the program continues on today with internal coaches leading the groups.

This program was the pilot for me and allowed me to get the experience and credibility in an industry and with group coaching. The price point has changed dramatically, but that opportunity gave me the launch that has allowed me to be extremely successful in my coaching business while giving me the flexibility to do other things I love.

Form an alliance with your existing clients or colleagues and offer coaching opportunities that neither of you could offer alone but both of you can attract clients together. Attorneys, accountants, financial planners, and sales professionals can share amazing facilities and clients. Focus on the value of creating coaching groups as a follow-up.

Example from a 12 Keys mentoring group: Joci using everyday contacts to form groups.
Joci was excited about coaching in groups but wasn't interested public speaking or starting a newsletter or creating teleforums. She decided to use advocates and key connections in her everyday network to create groups.

She formed a group with a dentist who was her individual client. After Joci and her client identified that her biggest problem was having high staff turnover, lack of staff enthusiasm, and an office environment that was not ideal for her patients, Joci offered to coach a brown-bag luncheon coaching group for the staff once a week, to teach and coach the staff on how to interact and communicate with the dentist's patients and each other more professionally and effectively. The result of this three-month coaching experiment was an amazing transformation in the office environment and staff enthusiasm. The dentist was so pleased with the results that she recommended Joci to other dentists in the dental association, which resulted in a chain of referrals for her groups.

The second advocate she contacted was her accountant. After hearing her accountant talk about how isolated she felt as a sole proprietor, Joci asked her if she knew any other accountants who felt the same way. When she said yes, Joci introduced the idea of creating a group of accountants who could meet in a coaching group and create a collegial environment to connect and share experiences.

Joci approached the manager of a spa where she was a member and had attended regularly for the past eight years. She proposed the idea for two free personal development workshops as an added value that the spa could offer to their membership. One workshop was offered after work hours and the other during the day. The manager of the spa was delighted and turned over the membership list to Joci so she could contact the clientele about the workshops. While holding the free three-hour workshop, Joci promoted coaching groups to those interested in implementing the personal growth and self-care strategies.

Joci said, "I don't see the advantage of creating new contacts when I have done business with so many professionals in my life. I am simply going to contact those people in my existing network and give them the opportunity to become advocates for my group coaching business." I loved her spunk and attitude and was thrilled over her success in starting her first coaching groups.

One of the most important concepts about marketing coaching was in Phoenix at a coaching conference that Thomas Leonard produced. One of the women in the audience shared her key concept about attracting clients into groups. She said it is important that we "Market specifically and coach generally." I immediately adopted that concept. As coaches, whether we coach individuals, groups, or teams, we are going to show up as the coach, so we will be coaching generally in whatever setting we are in. The key then is to market specifically to our ideal clients.

When I transitioned out of my real estate tax company and into coaching in 1995, I had no idea who my ideal clients would be. I was so excited about coaching that I talked to everyone I knew about what I was doing. During an annual review, my financial advisor asked about my career move, and I shared with him the new profession of coaching and how excited I was about finishing my coaching training. He said his managing partner had a coach in Canada and that he was interested in having a coach himself. He was one of my first clients and within three months he invited me to join his company study group for lunch. From that meeting, I added three new clients. And, one of the new clients was a woman who had high aspirations to grow her business and increase her production. Within three years, she was not only the top-producing woman in the company, but also had stepped up to a national leadership role in the organization. She became a tremendous advocate for coaching and for my business. From her introductions came the opportunity for me to start group coaching in that company that created ten coaching groups.

My ideal clients are financial services professionals, who have filled my coaching groups over the past fourteen years. You can develop a system for identifying and marketing to your ideal clients.

Case Study—Leveraging Advocates to Market and Implement a Group Coaching Program

Carol Heady completed the 12 Keys Mentoring Group in 2008

My client is a community bank located in upstate New York, a publicly traded company with more than three hundred employees. The CEO, who joined the company in 2005, set a new vision and mission for the bank and developed a strategic plan that included a goal specific to increasing the quality of service to its clients and build a sales and service culture. To achieve this goal, the company hired my company, Learning and Performance Solutions (LPS), in 2006 to perform a needs analysis to help determine and improve the service culture. Two members of the nine-member senior management team committed to improving the sales and service performance of the bank recognized that coaching was the single most effective method to improve overall performance. At the end of 2008, I met with the two members of the senior management team and proposed a group coaching model that would reinforce and support coaching behaviors, and increase the coaching effectiveness of the retail division branch managers. Over the course of these three years, both senior managers became my advocates, and in the beginning of 2009 they arranged a meeting with the CEO. In a matter of fifteen minutes he agreed to establish a group coaching program for the retail division branch managers.

As a result of the outcomes of the initial branch manager group, there were increased teller sales, more referrals received, more cross-selling opportunities developed, increased self confidence of the group participants, and more open internal communication. As a result of these excellent results, two additional branch manager groups were launched. The regional manager of the retail division and two branch managers became my advocates and advocates of group coaching and "sold" the program to the human resources director. Recently, a fourth group has been launched with non-branch managers.

A key lesson for me: My internal advocates marketed and sold the expansion of the branch managers' program. In this particular case, it was the "layering" of advocates that was both unexpected and extremely powerful in expanding the program to managers and supervisors outside the retail division of the bank.

Marketing strategy lessons: I started with existing clients, and deepened those relationships (in layers) so that I had multiple advocates across different functional and business lines. I also collected and shared specific outcomes and results to the company. I spoke with confidence as I marketed from a position of strength and credibility, knowing I had strong internal advocates who supported me. Leveraging advocates was budget friendly for my company while increasing revenues exponentially. Advocates built credibility for my group coaching programs, so the groups have sold themselves.

Carol A Heady, President
Learning and Performance Solutions
carol@learningandperformance.net
www.learningandperformance.net

Coaching Questions:
1. Do you have ideal clients that you would relish having in a coaching group?
2. Do you show up regularly in organizations where your ideal clients gather? In person and on the Web?
3. Are you visible with your clients? Do you speak, present, or write articles targeted to your ideal client?
4. Do you have advocates that will help you in your quest to create a group coaching business? Are you committed to helping them achieve their goals and dreams?
5. Do you always interview and get feedback from your ideal clients before you make a group coaching offering?

Chapter Sixteen
Designing a Group Coaching Business

"Whatever you can do or dream you can, begin it. Boldness has genius, power, and magic in it. Begin it now."
—J. W. von Goethe

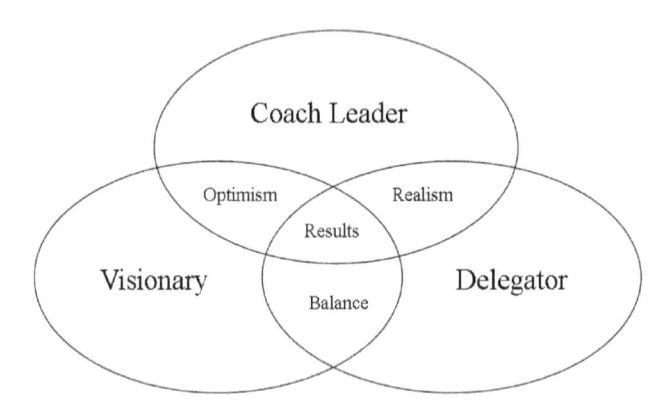

[Venn diagram with three overlapping circles labeled "Coach Leader", "Visionary", and "Delegator", with intersecting regions labeled "Optimism", "Realism", "Results", and "Balance"]

How to create a group coaching business that is successful and sustainable

It was an important frame of reference to recognize that a coaching business requires a dedicated and inspired CEO. Shifting my perspective away from having a coaching practice to embracing the concept of setting up a coaching business was a key awareness that encouraged me to create a business model. I attended an entrepreneurial program at the Cox School of Business at Southern Methodist University after I moved from education into running a property tax business in 1990, so when I stepped fully into a coaching business in 1997, I had some training and expertise in running a business. Some coach training schools include business courses to help coaches who have not run their own businesses to transition into entrepreneurship. The starting point is to recognize that a business can't be successful without an inspired CEO who is a visionary. This CEO can provide the momentum, the imagination, the catalyst for change, the innovation, and the leadership that keeps a business relevant, vital, and profitable. These are some key traits for the entrepreneurial coach:

- **Responsible**—personal responsibility to the operation of the business creates the basis for economic security and growth; it is up to the CEO to show up and begin it now.
- **Accountable**—being responsible to someone else. I have only been without a coach for three months in the last fifteen years. It is important for me to complete a coaching prep form each week that includes the opportunities, plans, choices, and intentions I have for my business. This gives me CEO time each week that encourages me to commit to a plan and follow through. It is also important to be accountable for my personal development and continue growing in that arena. Having a coach is invaluable in this process.
- **Visionary**—Garry Schleifer is the publisher of the outstanding coaching magazine, *Choice*, because he looked up and noticed that the coaching industry didn't have a magazine and got busy creating his outstanding publication. The CEO of a coaching business looks both internally and externally to envision what the next opportunity is available for the company.
- **Delegator**—creating a strong and capable team. "If you have a dream you can do by yourself, it's not a big enough dream. (anon.)" In this Internet age, there are multiple means for delegating operations to others that are inexpensive or even free.
- **Connector**—building alliances with partners in organizations, companies, and with other coaches and entrepreneurs to create social and economic capital and create business opportunities.
- **Optimistic**—as the pendulum swings from highs to lows in economic and business cycles, an entrepreneur must be up for the challenge and optimistic about the future. That optimism prevents him or her from getting stuck and losing momentum as he or she leads their team through these cycles.
- **Realistic**—as a counterbalance for optimism, an entrepreneur must be up to speed with the latest trends, opportunities, and hazards ahead for the business. Running a lean business machine, staying relatively debt free, and poised to make a move when an opportunity arrives are the hallmarks of effective entrepreneurism.

Top Ten Ways to Build an Entrepreneurial Group Coaching Business

1. Become CEO of your company. Work "on your business," not just "in your business." (Michael Gerber, *The EMyth Revisited*)
2. Create rich and valuable social capital by connecting regularly with other coaches, clients, colleagues, business professionals, and other entrepreneurs. Becoming a linchpin in your network allows you to volunteer, contribute, share contacts, be the host of a network, and have meaningful conversations with exceptional people.
3. Attract and connect with CEOs and entrepreneurial clients, and grow your business as they grow theirs.
4. Use your time wisely. Have CEO time, production time, and playtime scheduled. All are essential for growing your group coaching business.
5. Use your vast resources. Develop a menu of all the things available to you and use them to learn and know more and keep up with the latest trends and research.
6. Use mentoring and coaching to grow and sustain your business. One of the most effective ways to grow your business is to give away incredible value to others. Being generous with your time and resources as you coach and grow creates more abundance. It is important to refer business to others coaches. Knowing their ideal clients allows the opportunity to serve other coaches as well as helping potential clients find the best coach for them. It creates an incredible sense of abundance to refer business regularly.
7. Invest in your business. In order to succeed, you must put the time, energy, and resources in place in your business. Make sure you have up-to-date technology and an attractive office. Join associations and organizations where your ideal clients show up.
8. Create value for others and share it generously with as many people as possible. Learn the magic word, "NO." You can do anything you want; you just can't do everything you want. Choose wisely for what is meaningful to yourself and your business.
9. Have CEO meetings at least quarterly to make sure you are creating the vision and next steps for your business. These meetings cannot take place in your own office, because of the limitations of your familiar and task-oriented work space. Find an opulent venue that inspires you and engages your right brain as well as your left. My clients have retreated to a cabin in the mountains, to a cabana on Hawaiian seashore, to the top floor of a building in London, and

to a local tea shop. Find that spot that fully engages your brain. I love to go to a boardroom at a local five-star hotel and plan as if I am the CEO of a major international company. (I often invite my husband to join me for dinner at the five-star restaurant in the hotel to celebrate the next step in my visionary plan.) Operating from abundance makes you irresistible to clients and business opportunities.

10. Once you have stepped into the CEO role, it is time to put a business model in place for your coaching business and get experience coaching individual clients. It is time to expand your business into group coaching. At this point, you have identified your ideal clients, and now it is time to attract them into groups with you.

Design a group coaching model. I mentor coaches individually and in groups to help them design and implement sustainable group coaching models.

Here is an example of an excellent coach who designed her business model in 2003 and has implemented it successfully for years. I am enclosing the key elements she created in the 12 Keys Program in 2003.

Denise Cormier's Group Coaching Business Model
Denise Cormier set up from the beginning to launch her group coaching business with a business model and specific goals in place. As a result, group coaching has been an integral part of her business. Her website is a great place to check out her successful group offerings that have flourished for these last seven years (www.cormierassociates.com).

Vision: Develop a coaching business that provides me with stable and secure income of six figures or more, balance for work and life pursuits and loves, and the opportunity to use and leverage my creativity, ingenuity, and coaching and consulting skills while having fun and being stimulated.

Business Development Goals:
1. Secure current work possibilities in order to concentrate on developing coaching business.
2. Envision and focus on coaching services—group and individual—in every conversation with work and personal networks.
3. Get five coaching groups started by June 30, 2003
   - Identify and begin marketing coaching groups in the corporate setting.

- Explore financial group coaching idea.
- Explore women's business leaders coaching group.
- Explore team leaders coaching groups.
- Identify network for collecting coaching groups.
- Explore human resource managers coaching groups.
4. Explore e-change opportunity.
5. Work with my coach to streamline my process for setting up a successful coaching practice.
6. Revise website to take advantage of new ideas and opportunities:
    - Get price quotes for making changes.
    - Identify hosting possibilities so all mail is at Cormier Associates.
    - Identify whether I won or can get www.cormierassociates.com.
7. Identify creative business services that leverage my experiences.
8. Identify creative marketing strategies for specific services.
    - Workshop presentation on creating the perfect life.
9. Constantly improve my coaching skills: take the individual SOC advanced proficiency classes and listen to live coaching.
10. Identify coaching areas and ideal clients:
    - Groups, managers, leaders, team leaders: project teams, virtual teams, IS teams. MD teams, HR change agents, women leaders: CEOs, EDs, executive directors, physicians.
11. Work with my coach to streamline my process for setting up a successful coaching practice.

Denise Cormier
Cormier Associates
Denise@cormierassociates.com
www.cormierassociates.com

It takes courage and passion to step up and become the CEO of a fledgling group coaching business. It is not for the faint of heart, but the rewards and experiences you will have are extraordinary. By heading up a successful group coaching business, you will experience the joy of partnering with people in groups of peers and supporting them through the opportunities, challenges, and struggles in their lives and watch them emerge confidently and successfully moving ahead in their lives is an amazing experience.

"I never cease to be amazed at the power of the coaching process to draw out the skills or talent that was previously hidden within an individual, and which invariable finds a way to solve a problem previously thought unsolvable."

—John Russell, managing director of Harley-Davidson Europe, Ltd.

> **Coaching Questions:**
> 1. What is the vision for your coaching business?
> 2. Do you have a business model and plan?
> 3. Do you schedule CEO time regularly to explore business opportunities and evaluate the current status of your business?
> 4. Are you keeping up with the changes and trends in your industry and with the economy in general?
> 5. Are you making strong alliances and creating advocates to help you build and grow your business?

About the Author

Ginger Cockerham, MCC, is an Executive Business Coach, who has an international group coaching business that includes executives and professionals in financial, corporate, and service industries. Some of the organizations where she has coached individuals and groups are Northwestern Mutual Financial Network, Farmers Insurance, Fortis Bank Global, New York Life, The Texas Rangers baseball team, Hughes and Luce, Editorial Intelligence (UK), and Women in Insurance and Financial Services.

Ginger is a Master Certified Coach with the International Coach Federation and served on the board of directors for five years and as vice president of ICF in 2007 and 2008. She presently serves on the Board of Trustees for the ICF Foundation, where the mission is to provide resources for coaching companies who support educational leaders worldwide. She is on the faculty at the University of Texas Dallas and Coach University. She teaches a group coaching course at Columbia University and a group coaching training program at Coachville.

Ginger has presented to international conferences and organizations on the topic of group coaching for many years and is recognized as an expert in the field of peer group coaching.

As a columnist for the London Times in 2008, Ginger wrote a biweekly coaching column read worldwide. She is the author of *Group Coaching:*

A Comprehensive Blueprint, and *Magnificent Masters in Financial Services.* Her CD series, *Creating, Collecting and Coaching Groups,* is a best seller in the coaching industry. She has been featured in the *London Times,* the *Chicago Tribune, Choice* magazine, *Fort Worth Star Telegram, Richmond Times-Dispatch, GAMA International Journal,* and *Health* magazine.